THE STOIC PATH

TIMELESS WISDOM FOR THE MODERN WORLD

DYLAN WINTON

ANNUS MIRABILIS
PUBLISHING

© Copyright 2023 Dylan Winton - All rights reserved.

The content contained within this book may not be reproduced, duplicated, or transmitted without direct written permission from the author or the publisher.

Under no circumstances will any blame or legal responsibility be held against the publisher, or author, for any damages, reparation, or monetary loss due to the information contained within this book. Either directly or indirectly.

Legal Notice

This book is copyright protected. This book is only for personal use. You cannot amend, distribute, sell, use, quote or paraphrase any part, or the content within this book, without the consent of the author or publisher.

Disclaimer Notice

Please note the information contained within this document is for educational and entertainment purposes only. All effort has been executed to present accurate, up to date, and reliable, complete information. No warranties of any kind are declared or implied. Readers acknowledge that the author is not engaging in the rendering of legal, financial, medical or professional advice. The content within this book has been derived from various sources. Please consult a licensed professional before attempting any techniques outlined in this book.

By reading this document, the reader agrees that under no circumstances is the author responsible for any losses, direct or indirect, which are incurred as a result of the use of the information contained within this document, including, but not limited to, — errors, omissions, or inaccuracies.

CONTENTS

Introduction v

1. A Trip Back To The Start 1
2. The Principles And Pillars 9
3. The Promise 17
4. Life And Death 23
5. Mindset And Perspective 31
6. Business Stoics 60
7. What Others Think Of Stoicism 68
8. Preparing Yourself For Practice 80
9. The Practices 84

Afterword 97

INTRODUCTION

Stoicism is a philosophical concept that people throughout the ages have found intriguing and about which they have sought out more information. Philosophy is a complex field, but many of the principles set down by those who lived long ago still influence us today. The Stoic philosophy in particular holds many secrets that can help us tackle many of the issues that pop up in our modern lives.

Stoicism is a philosophy that originated with the ancient Greeks and survives even today. If you're yearning to learn about something that could help you take control of your life, Stoicism might be the answer, so let's get started.

This book will teach you how to emulate the characteristics of the ancient Stoics. It will imbue you with their wisdom, resilience, self-discipline, confidence, calmness, critical thinking, and decision-making ability. Most importantly, you'll learn how to take control of your life by using the ancient Stoics' teachings. This journey won't be easy, but I'm confident you will find your way through it and be successful.

My name is X, and I have spent years learning and studying various religions, beliefs and cultures. For 10 years, I immersed myself in learning and speaking with experts about the Hellenistic philosophy known as Stoicism, which was founded by philosopher Zeno of Citium.

I can honestly say its practices and methods have changed my life, so I decided to write a book to teach others how to use it to change theirs.

This book will teach anyone who is unaware of Stoicism what its purpose is, and I'll share my own and others' views about it, so you can develop your own opinion about how useful it can be in your life.

From my perspective, the Stoic philosophy has endured the test of time and is the ideal philosophy to help us take control of our life. It can also ensure that you are able to deal with emotions in the most productive way possible.

At this point, you might be wondering why I feel so strongly about the value of the Stoic philosophy and why I want to pass on my knowledge to you, so I'll begin with a personal story.

You see, I used to be extremely introverted. If I could've stayed indoors for the rest of my life, I would have. My life was passing me by. Before learning about Stoicism, I wasn't interested in much, and I also let other people trample over me. But after applying Stoic teachings to my life, I became someone new.

I finally developed a social life, and even a love life! I started a business, and its growth rate has shocked me. This gave me time to write, and to learn more about various religions and philosophies.

My family and others who know me were astounded at the dramatic shift my life had taken. But trust me when I say, *This can happen to you too!*

I understand being skeptical, but I promise that this book will unlock abilities you didn't even know you had, and not even a week after you've finished it, doors will be opening all around you.

Every second spent not knowing how to control your mind is another second of your mind being limited and another second of life wasted. Stop being the person who procrastinates. Learn to live, be, and thrive in the moment with the teachings of the Stoics. These teachings will help you accomplish any goal on Earth, whether that's finding your dream job, boosting your career, attracting romance or just achieving a sports goal. Stoicism can help with just about everything!

The Stoic teachings that you are about to learn have been used and have worked for over 2,000 years now. In fact, they've even been refined since the days of the ancient Greeks.

Every chapter in this book will provide you with teachings through quotes, strategies or step-by-step plans to force out old habits and ways of doing things and replace them with valuable knowledge of Stoicism and new ways of behaving. My hope is that this book will enhance not only your mindset but your chances of getting what you want out of life and enjoying every moment.

The first step to taking control of your life is right in front of you, and all you need to do is continue reading.

1

A TRIP BACK TO THE START

Stoicism was first introduced during the Hellenistic period. Its name comes from the porch (stoa poikilê) of the Agora (public space used for assemblies) in Athens, where its founder, Zenon of Citium, lectured. Here, members of the Stoic school gathered and held their lectures.

The Stoics held to the opinion that feelings such as fear, envy, or intense love for anything were harmful to the human condition. They believed that these emotions arise from false judgments, and that an enlightened, intellectual person would not succumb to them. It is the goal of Stoicism to attain such a state, and one who has done so is referred to as a sage.

This state of contentment is called *eudaimonia*. According to ancient Stoics, it is attained by living in harmony with all other living things. This means both satisfying our roles in the universe as a whole, and living as a human being.

Later, in Roman times, these doctrines were emphasized. The sage was said to be immune to misfortune, for they are unaffected by the emotions named above. The Roman Stoics found that this was enough to be happy.

According to Stoics, philosophy is much like a living creature, with logic being its bones, and ethics and physics its body and soul. A more modern perspective suggests that ethics is the soul, while physics is the body.

According to Stoics, human beings are different from all other living creatures because they are able to reason and think, and humans should live in accord with this reason. In order to attain eudaimonia, we must live not in accordance with our passions, but with reason (a state of mind called *apatheia*).

You might be wondering how this affects things beyond our control. Well, according to Stoics, the events outside our control should have no bearing on our well-being.

Let's take a look at ancient Stoics; they lived between 300 BC and 200 AD. This period has been divided by historians into three phases: early, middle, and late stoa.

EARLY STOA

Stoicism started with the thoughts of Zeno of Citium. Around 300 BC, Zeno decided to stand against Epicureanism, and its founder, Epicurus. They believed that the world is materialistic, that the universe was an accident, and that the absence of pain and fear consitute the greatest pleasure. Zeno developed Stoicism in order to stand in stark contrast to this concept and took from the Cynic ideas positing that virtue and simplicity were the highest values.

Zeno laid the building blocks of early Stoicism. He maintained that the Stoic philosophy would emphasize three areas: physics, logic, and ethics. While today's Stoics mostly concern themselves with ethics, Zeno believed that there was no ethics without its two supporting pillars - physics and logic.

When Zeno died in 262 BC, he was succeeded by Cleanthes, his best pupil, who was head of the Stoic school for 32 years, until his death in 230 BC.

MIDDLE STOA

The middle stoa begins in 100 BC. During this time period, the center of Stoic teaching had moved away from Athens, and found a new home in Rhodes, Greece. Panaetius was the 7th leader of Stoic thought, and he presented a major shift from Zeno. He found ways to simplify the ideas of Stoics, especially those concerning physics. During his time, Stoicism moved far closer to Neoplatonism (the school of thought rooted in the philosophy of Plato but extending beyond it). This shift also brought Stoicism to ancient Rome.

Due to Panaetius' more eclectic style, and the spreading of Stoicism, it was no longer unified under one banner.

This period also gave us perhaps the most representative Stoic of them all - Cato the Younger. Cato was uncompromising and strict in his beliefs, much closer to Zeno than Panaetius.

LATE STOA

The late stoa is very much a time period dominated by interest in ethics. Logic and physics, despite Zeno's insistence on their importance, were largely forgotten. Despite this, the late stoa is the period when Stoic thought was at its highest. It is also the only time period from which we have full works available.

One of these comes from Seneca the Younger. Seneca opted to use everyday happenings in order to debate moral issues in his book, *Moral Letters to Lucilius*. This personal style of writing influenced not only philosophy, but also literature for the coming centuries. If you're looking to read a Stoic work, you can't go wrong with Seneca the Younger, as his works are extremely accessible even in this day and age.

On the other side of this, there's possibly the best introduction to Stoicism written by an ancient Stoic – a short manual by Epictetus entitled *Enchiridion*. Despite Epictetus himself being born a slave, he ascended to the philosophical thought of his time in ways that most of his contemporaries would find beyond them.

As a testament to how influential Stoic philosophy was, we have Marcus Aurelius, who becam a Roman emperor, but never lost his philosopher's heart. He pursued Stoic ideals in every facet of his life, and many attribute this as the reason his rule was so successful. Even centuries after his death, some of his works remain and are critical Stoic reading material. In true Stoic fashion, he even refused to choose an heir, believing that the most suitable should rule Rome, whether it be his flesh and blood or not.

Not all rulers shared Marcus' love for Stoicism. During Nero's time (Roman emperor from 54-68 AD), it was strictly forbidden to preach Stoicism, and yet men like Gaius Musonius Rufus did it anyway. This led to Rufus being exiled from Rome, which he took with the dignity that only a Stoic could have.

Now, we've talked about the Stoics of the old ages, but I hear you asking, "How can a philosophy that is 2,000 years old possibly work in the modern day?"

But if we think about Christianity and Buddhism, for example, these are also philosophies over 2,000 years old that are still practiced today. The difference is that Stoicism preaches far less and doesn't cling idly to the idea of an Abrahamic god.

The ideas of Stoicism are still relevant, and may in fact be more relevant than ever. After all, in times of war, the well-being of an individual is scarcely thought of. On the other hand, we are currently in a time of relative peace. The modern world is all about making yourself as happy as possible.

Today, Stoicism is undergoing a revival among the people, but why is that?

Let us begin with the most important teaching of Stoicism - the difference between things that are within our control and those that aren't. At a fundamental level, what does being unhappy about things outside of our control do? Well, it doesn't do anything, does it?

For example, no matter how much you despair about aging, it will not stop the process. According to Stoic thought, these things should be simply left to pass, and we should focus on the things we can affect. How much energy do you spend worrying about what others think? What they may tweet about you? What might or might not happen to you in the future, or even what could have been changed in the past?

Now imagine if you spent all that energy on something productive. That is the essence of Stoicism.

Leaving behind things you cannot affect will bring you close to what Stoics call their 'inner character.' The pursuit of this is worth almost everything to the Stoic. The pursuit of virtue, in the end, is most important.

All external things—fame, money, power over others—they're all what a Stoic would call "indifferent."

According to Stoic thought, nothing but your own state of mind can affect whether you're happy or not. A person does not cater to the whims of their brain, their brain caters to their whims.

All we need to do is teach ourselves this concept. Now, I understand that this is a pretty foreign idea. After all, you've been brought up to respect and cherish these other things. But this book will slowly guide you, step by step, until you can sufficiently understand Stoic reasoning and apply it to yourself.

Do you want more money? Yes, of course you do. After all, doesn't everyone? Have you ever asked yourself why you want more money? The answer may seem obvious: "To buy things, why else?" But why are you buying things? I believe all of us would agree that it is to make ourselves happy. But why do we need things to make us happy? After all, happiness is merely a state of mind, and aren't there people who are happy without those things?

For example, the Aboriginals in Australia are happy without the newest iPhone. This is because they value different things, like strength, or maybe hunting or singing skills.

One key thing to understsand is that improvement is not necessary for happiness. All you need to value is your own virtue as a human being. Some might ask, "But why?" Well, why not? Is there a reason to experience the harm that is unhappiness?

I am not suggesting that you abandon all worldly pursuits. What I am telling you is to abandon the idea that you need material goods in order to be happy.

Let's review an example. You've gone to court over a speeding ticket, you know you weren't speeding, and the evidence is in your favor. Despite that, the cop that came to the hearing is the judge's brother. As a result, you are told you must pay for a crime you did not commit.

A non-Stoic person would become stressed by this injustice. Of course it's unfair, but does it matter? A Stoic would simply consider the fact that they were unable to affect the outcome of the situation, and move on, not letting it affect them in the slightest.

Weirdly enough, even though Stoicism teaches us to care less about worldly pursuits, learning Stoicism can actually make you more successful.

The first benefit is, naturally, improved mental health. You'll be a lot better mentally if you aren't worrying about things you don't need to. You'll also develop a firmer, stronger mindset.

Beyond that, you'll gain greater confidence. My insecurities in youth came from concerning myself far too much with others' opinions about me. A true Stoic would be entirely unfazed by this.

Another benefit is increased success. Confident people are generally seen as more responsible, which tends to lead to greater professional success. Furthermore, if you don't concern yourself with office politics and other distractions, you'll move up the ladder much faster.

Honestly, Stoicism even saved my love life! I used to approach girls once in a blue moon, and I would be crippled for months on end after being rejected. Once I developed a Stoic mindset, the rejections didn't faze me, and women found my newfound confidence much more attractive.

2

THE PRINCIPLES AND PILLARS

Stoicism is a philosophical concept characterized by specific ethical notions of what Stoics believe to be facts about the world, and pillars that describe our ways of tackling the world - characteristics a sage, or enlightened individual, should possess.

In this chapter, we'll be exploring these principles and pillars, as well as their importance and application to our lives.

THE PRINCIPLES

Nature

This principle states that "nature is rational." In other words, nature behaves rationally and abides by the laws of physics.

This principle prevents us from thinking that nature "hates us" or that it acts randomly. How many times have you cursed the world for something that happened seemingly at random? Most of us have done this quite often. But Stoics do not. This principle also helps us understand the world around us.

By observing this principle, we avoid the pitfalls of many modern religious philosophies that claim to have omnipotent gods. Rather, we accept nature at face value, knowing that it doesn't act with an agenda, but simply acts according to reason. Things like aging, bad weather and death are part of nature and are not designed to harm us, so there is no point in raging against them.

Law of reason

This principle states that the universe itself is governed by either a law, or multiple laws from which no one can escape. This can be further extended to say that human societies are all governed by laws based on nature, and goes further than just the laws of physics.

This principle states that it is intrinsic to the human condition for us to obey these natural laws. This principle is important if we as a society are to avoid anarchy. Understanding that humans must obey certain laws outside of their control helps stop anarchist ideals in their tracks.

Virtue

Here's a hot one! All Stoics agree that the principle here is that a life led in accordance to rational nature is a virtuous one. The "rational nature" here is not the rational nature from the first principle, however, but refers to the rational nature of humankind. In other words, a human is a creature of reason and all our actions and decisions should be sparked not by emotion, but by reason. This is possibly one of the hardest principles to show, because it goes against many of our modern-day principles.

Helping a homeless person because you pity them, for example, would not be virtuous for a Stoic. A Stoic's way of approaching the situation is to help them so they may more easily better themselves, in turn improving the society you both live in.

This idea is quite practical in our daily lives, since it forces us to question our decisions and determine where they're coming from. We may often catch ourselves acting based on emotion, but our inner Stoic will hopefully stop us.

Wisdom

The principle of wisdom is a bit less practical than the others we've mentioned so far and speaks to a deeper subject. This principle states that wisdom is the cardinal, root virtue, and that insight, bravery, self-control, and justice spawn from it.

"But isn't bravery spawned from emotion?" you might ask. No. In fact, bravery is the act of conquering a strong emotion in favor of rational thought.

This principle isn't very practical. You won't be thinking of it every day, but it does help put things into perspective. It teaches us that the pursuit of wisdom is virtuous, and reminds us of the most important characteristics of it.

Apatheia

This principle states that since passion is irrational, and intrinsic to humans, our lives should be lived as a battle against passion, and that we should avoid intense feelings.

This is the principle of Stoicism most embodied in modern-day representations.

This is, in my opinion, the most crucial principle to master. It connects well to the aforementioned virtue of self-control. It is, at the same time, the one that seems most contrary to human nature. After all, it might seem that a life without passion is empty. Quite the contrary, however; passion is much like a drug.

An individual on heroin is happy, but are they virtuous? Most of us might say that no, they are not virtuous, because to obtain that happiness, they have injected their body with a poison. Passion, to Stoics, is worse: it is a poison to the mind.

This principle is best referenced in daily life in a moment when one would act out rashly. Most things that we regret have come from emotion, but adhering to the principle of apathiea would stop us from behaving this way.

Pleasure

The idea that pleasure is good seems like a no-brainer to most of us. But the principle of pleasure states that pleasure has no intrinsic value; it is neither good nor bad. On the other hand, it is only considered to be acceptable if it doesn't get in the way of the pursuit of virtue. The moment pleasure interferes with virtue is the moment it becomes bad.

In other words, this principle warns against decadence and hedonism. Living for pleasure is to live a hollow shell of a life, never truly coming close to the reason we exist. It is living an irrational, forgettable life, though one that has been lived by countless before you.

Pleasure isn't bad, so don't think you're doing something bad if you feel good. On the other hand, if you find yourself binge-watching your third Netflix show instead of working or taking care of household chores, it might be time to re-evaluate your priorities.

Evil

The principle of evil is difficult to comprehend, but it is integral to the understanding of Stoicism. It states that poverty, illness, and even death, are not evil. Let's clarify this concept.

Much like pleasure is not good simply because it feels good, poverty and illness are not bad simply because they feel bad. Instead, they are extensions of the rational nature, meaning that they are natural consequences of the human condition.

This can help us more easily come to terms with things that we perceive as negative. Stoicism teaches us that instead of falling into a depression when a loved one dies, we should pull ourselves up by the bootstraps and rise to the occasion.

Duty

Why, you may ask, do we even seek virtue? This principle is the answer. It states that the pursuit of virtue should never be conducted for pleasure, but rather for the duty that comes with being human.

Humans are the only animals capable of reason, and from this follows that we're the only ones capable of pursuing virtue. Would it not be a waste for us to fail to seek virtue? Are we not compelled to do it, by the sheer fact that we are human?

Pursuing virtue for the sake of pleasure is, in fact, one of the least Stoic things one can do. While the pursuit of wisdom is virtuous, it is only virtuous if it is done for the right reasons.

THE PILLARS

Acceptance

Stoic acceptance is the pillar that governs our acceptance of what is outside of our own control. The mind is a feeble thing, and it will drone on endlessly about the future, or worse, the past. We've all spent hours thinking about things that have happened, things that will happen, or things that might happen.

> *"True happiness is to enjoy the present, without anxious dependence upon the future, not to amuse ourselves with either hopes or fears but to rest satisfied with what we have, which is sufficient, for he that is so wants nothing."*
>
> — SENNECA

This quote instructs us to live in the present moment. We must not live in the future or the past, but in the present. Oftentimes, we will be negatively affected by the actions of others, but these are actions we couldn't control.

> *"When you run up against someone else's shamelessness, ask yourself this: Is a world without shamelessness possible? No. Then don't ask the impossible."*
>
> — MARCUS AURELIUS

Aurelius teaches us that we should do what we can about the things that are, rather than complain about that which is not possible.

Awareness

The pillar of awareness is built upon Stoic acceptance. It is the idea that our minds are creating suffering and explains that we need to take responsibility for our own thoughts.

A lack of awareness is exhibited when we are concerned with others' opinions, or trivial things like status. These are not the things causing us suffering; we would not suffer if we did not believe them to be important. But rather than focusing on these things, we should focus on our own thoughts and actions.

To take control of yourself is to stand face to face with reality. We often add our own judgments to stories, people, and events. Rather than doing this, we need to understand that our thoughts are not reality. In the words of Epictetus:

> *"Practice saying to every harsh appearance: You are an appearance, and in no manner what you appear to be."*

Action

The last two pillars of Stoicism concern the mind of the Stoic. The third, action, focuses its attention on acting on the world. The first two pillars are fundamentally pointless unless they are coupled with acting on them.

> *"Waste no more time arguing about what a good man should be. Be one."*

> — *MARCUS AURELIUS*

If there was only one quote from this book to commit to mind, it would be this one. You control yourself; every single aspect of your behavior is entirely under your control. You can act wisely or emotionally; it is completely your choice. It is a choice in parts, so many small habits finally cumulate into a personality.

We need to not only resolve to act with wisdom, but also to take responsibility for those times when we do not. It's easy to become distracted by the world, but we need to stay focused.

Antifragility

What is antifragility? Is it the same as being resilient, or strong? Not quite. To be a true Stoic is to take the stressors of life and make them a driving force.

This is why Stoics have earned the nickname "Buddhists with an attitude." I would add hair to that description, but other than that, I agree! To be antifragile is to take a negative action and, instead of questioning how to make it disappear, question how we can use it to drive ourselves to action. Once we've found our answer, there's little else to do than to simply act.

While acceptance of what we're unable to affect is crucial to the Stoic, one could argue that taking it in stride and making it help us act is even more important. Instead of leaning too hard into acceptance, learn to be antifragile.

You might have noticed that many of these principles and pillars blend into one another, but that's because they come from the same fundamental place: the pursuit of virtue.

3

THE PROMISE

"Happiness and freedom begin with a clear understanding of one principle: Some things are within our control, and some things are not. It is only after you have forced up to this fundamental rule and learned to distinguish between what you can and can't control that inner tranquility and outer effectiveness become possible."

— EPICTETUS

Epictetus promises us that studying Stoicism can offer practical tools that we can apply in our life in order to reach eudaimonia, which translates to doing or living well, or the highest human good to which we can strive.

The promise of Stoicism, in other words, is not happiness, but serenity, or a state of consciousness when one is satisfied with things as they are. This is how we can live a morally virtuous life. Zeno defined happiness as a "good flow of life." This means that our life runs smoothly when we live in harmony with ourselves and with the way things are.

Stoicism emphasizes characteristics such as honesty, moderation, resolve and self-discipline, justice, courage, and fortitude.

> *"How long are you going to wait before you demand the best for yourself?"*
>
> — *EPICTETUS*

Shouldn't inner tranquility be the goal of everyone? The core values of Stoicism, when practiced diligently, can lead to a better life you may not have even thought was possible.

When we understand what we have control over and what we don't, we spend more time and effort dealing with things we can control and less time worrying about things we can't. In his book, *A Guide to the Good Life: The Ancient Art of Stoic Joy*, professor of philosophy William B. Irvine offered an update to this Stoic idea of the dichotomy of control with his *trichotomy of control*. This modern theory suggests that there are things over which we have complete control (such as goals we set for ourselves), things over which we have no control (such as whether the sun rises tomorrow), and things over which we have some control (such as whether we win our tennis game tomorrow).

Let's think about a goal from this revised perspective of the trichotomy of control, dividing it into three parts. The first part is that which we have complete control over, such as how much time we spend learning how to improve our chances of achieving it, our feelings and thoughts about it, and how much work we put into it. The second part are those aspects that are only partially within our control, such as how prepared we are. Things are only partially within our control because they can be influenced by external factors, such as the difficulty of the goal and whether someone else is better prepared than us.

Finally, the third part consists of things out of our control. No matter how well we prepare for something, there can always be obstacles that get in our way, like the weather, an illness, world events, etc.

The Stoic philosophy posits that what we can control is our resilience and resourcefulness in the face of these challenges. By focusing on that which we can control, we spend no time worrying about what we can't control, and this leads to inner tranquility and outer effectiveness. We develop outer effectiveness because we have prepared and learned to the best of our abilities, and inner tranquility because we know that no matter what happens, we are now stronger, better and smarter than we were yesterday.

Wouldn't you love to have this inner peace and outer effectiveness in your life?

This state is possible when we take the time to direct our energy to those things which we can control in life, and move our efforts away from those things we cannot control. Respect your ability to control your thoughts and avoid false perceptions. Live in the present and appreciate the time you have on this planet.

You cannot control how other people treat you, for example, but you can control how you react to that treatment. You cannot control the weather, but you can choose to dance in the rain or go inside during a blizzard. We have no control over whether life will end tomorrow, but we can control how we live today.

If you have felt as if you are trying to move a mountain and yet nothing happens, it could be because you are focusing on the things you cannot change or control, and are spending too little energy on the things you can. Much of what we say and do are not necessary or essential to our lives, so when we eliminate it, we are actually saving energy for the more important stuff. Stoicism offers us the promise of courage and practical wisdom.

There is a beautiful metaphor offered by the Stoics about an archer. Imagine that you are an archer and you are trying to hit a target. What can you control? You can control your practice of archery, for hours and days, you can choose the best bows and arrows that are available to you and take good care of them, and you can focus up to the second you let the arrow go.

But after that, things are completely out of your control as the target can move or a gust of wind could ruin your best shot. You missed. This is the lesson of not attaching your self-esteem to the outcome, to whether or not you hit the mark, but only to your attempt to hit it.

A general rule of thumb regarding this concept of control is that most of the time the things that we can control begin with us, as we control our own mind and actions. The things that we cannot control are mostly outside factors, whether world events like a pandemic, the weather, or other people's emotions and behavior.

When it comes to partial control, a promotion at work is a good example. We can work hard and improve our own capabilities, but we can't control how prepared our competition is or the thoughts and emotions of the person making the decision about who to promote. But when we don't try, our chances for failure are a hundred percent.

Life in harmony with nature is a Stoic ethical ideal. It means living in harmony with your own nature, in accordance with the universe. Zeno tells us, "Life in harmony with nature, that is, living in virtue." The Stoic believes in a kind of determinism - that everything that happens has a cause that leads to an effect. But they also assert that even in a deterministic world, our actions are ultimately 'up to us.'

Ataraxia, or equanimity, is a state of peace and wellbeing characterized by lack of distress or outward displays of strong emotion. This state is considered by Stoics to be a by-product of one's pursuit of moral character.

Autarky is essentially the ideal of self-sufficiency or self-reliance, and Stoics believe one can find the contentment of ataraxia by focusing on internal resources rather than relying on external factors.

Basically, Stoicism tells us there are no good or bad happenings in life; it is all about our perception. This way of thinking is quite challenging, because how can we accept the death of a loved one, for example? No one wants to hear, "That's it, accept it." It can seem to us that this means "Give up," "Don't feel," or "Surrender."

But consider this from another angle: What is the opposite of acceptance? Denial or rejection. To deny the facts means to deny reality. The first step is to accept reality as it is.

Denial is irrational and will not change the circumstances. The Stoics say we need to accept the facts in order to know what to do with them. We must not cry over fate, but instead, move on.

Everything in life has an end and when you make peace with that, you start seeing the machinery of the world and the flow of life. Don't avert your gaze from painful experiences, look at them objectively and think about them. This is the Stoic's promise of breaking the illusion and facing the reality of disappointment, loss, death and false hopes.

4

LIFE AND DEATH

"Death smiles upon us all. All a man can do is smile back."

— *MARCUS AURELIUS*

Life and death are inseparable. It is important to note that these concepts are not opposites, but that death is part of life. Everyone dies. It is scary, it is the end and it mortifies us. No one wants to die, not even those who believe in heaven.

We take time for granted, assuming there will be more if it in the future. Stoics preach about not living life as if we have years and years ahead of us. Death could happen at any time; accidents, mass shootings, diseases; people are dying prematurely every single day. Everything is born to die.

The philosopher Seneca connected the time before birth to the time after death, stating that after death we become what we were before our birth, which is a beautiful way of completing the circle of life and death.

So, we know that life ends in death, but we avoid thinking about it. It is scary and unknown. But the day will come when all of us will no longer exist. Death should serve as a motivator to live the best and fullest life possible. There is no reason to fight or not accept what we cannot change.

> *"I have to die. If it is now, well then, I die now; if later, then now I will take my lunch, since the hour for lunch has arrived - and dying I will tend to later."*

— EPICTETUS

Here we see that Epictetus was blunt and had a sarcastic sense of humor. He chose not to worry about death, but to think about lunch. We all know we are going to die; that is not under our control - not when, how or where. But lunch, on the other hand, is very much within our control.

But Epictetus suggested one other, much darker scenario. Imagine, as you kiss your child goodnight, what would it be like if you woke up in the morning without them. This can happen, and tragically happens all the time. It is our lack of preparation for such a painful event that makes our experience even more distressing.

The Stoic philosophy suggests conquering the fear of death and seeing it from an objective point of view as a natural occurrence that we will all face at some point. Death is a recurring theme, regardless of class, culture, age, race, or religion, because all humans die.

People around us will die, and it will hurt, at times so much that it seems unbearable. Stoics practice remembering that we are mortal and using this as motivation or a compass that leads them to live life. Stoics practice thinking about death often, so they never forget how limited their time is.

Stoic philosophy is not about suppressing emotions, it is about learning how to face, process and handle emotions instead of running from them. Sit with your emotions, accept and process them. Remember, it is all part of life. You don't bury a friendship you had with a friend who has died, you bury the person.

> *"Let death and exile, and all other things which appear terrible, be daily before your eyes, but death chiefly; and you will never entertain an abject though, not too eagerly covet anything."*
>
> — EPICTETUS

The question about and realization of mortality was central in the Stoic mindset, as we can see from the advice to visualize death every day. But Epictetus is not saying we should be morose; on the contrary, he states that death only appears to be terrible.

The purpose of thinking about death daily is to realize that death is one of the facts of life, that it is inevitable. Recognizing this is powerful and can shape our decisions and beliefs concerning what is truly important and valuable in life.

Talking about mortality is not like talking about sports, current events or the latest fashion trend and it tends to strike a nerve, but it is part of the core of the human experience. We are living parts of the ever-changing universe and living in accord with the universe makes us wise and persuasive.

"It is not death that man should fear, but rather never beginning to live."

— MARCUS AURELIUS

Life comes and goes, beginning with birth and ending with death. Aurelius is urging us to live a full life. What will we do between birth and death? Are we really living this life? Is it vibrant and fulfilled?

Life is the greatest journey you will ever be on and it is up to you to live it the best you can. The things we want to accomplish, our beliefs, our goals, and our relationships are all parts of living. Thinking about death daily provokes us to think about life at the same time, to remember to genuinely live each day we have.

Living life knowing it's the only life we have is the wisest thing one can do. We are all different; what is good for one person won't necessarily be good for another. But living a full life doesn't mean that you should only make good decisions or not make mistakes. A full life is one that includes good and bad, salty and sweet, fortune and tragedy.

The Stoics believed that our goal in life should be living in harmony with nature, of which we are all part. We must experience both sides of life in a Stoic manner, with understanding that we have little to no control over much of what we experience. Living in harmony with "nature" refers to human nature that follows higher reasoning, not our base natural impulses, and for Stoics, this means being our best self.

"If it is endurable, then endure it. Stop complaining."

— MARCUS AURELIUS

It is in our nature to avoid the tragic and embrace the positive experiences. But this isn't how we should operate; we should embrace everything in a Stoic manner, with the understanding that we have very little control over what we experience.

Our wisdom begins when we recognize that these things will disturb our calm. Aurelius tells us to stop complaining. After all, what good has complaining done for anyone? Complaining is as natural to us as breathing, but it is merely an unnecessary act of describing something negatively without including productive next steps to rectify the problem.

Yes, venting your frustrations can be liberating, but it is not likely to change the situation for the better. In the end, the obstacle or difficulty is either endurable or it isn't. If you can handle what life has thrown at you, do not complain, since this will make things even more difficult for you. When we complain, negative thoughts take root and it makes a bad situation worse.

We are very good at noticing what doesn't work or what is wrong but the Stoic doesn't have time to complain, because there are many things they can improve. Again, it is about things you can and can't control. Only our own decisions, words, and actions are worthy of our efforts and attention, because these are the things we can control.

So, whenever you feel like complaining, take a step back, focus on the whole picture and find things you are grateful for. Now is the time to start living your ideals. How long can you afford to put off who you really want to be? Your nobler self cannot wait any longer. Put your principles into practice - now. Stop the excuses and procrastination.

This is your life! The sooner you commit yourself to your spiritual program, the happier you will be. The longer you wait, the more likely you are to live a life of mediocrity and to feel shame and regret, because you know you are capable of better.

> *"From this instant on, vow to stop disappointing yourself. Separate yourself from the mob. Decide to be extraordinary and do what you need to do – now."*
>
> — EPICTETUS

You have to assemble your life by yourself. The sooner you devote yourself to doing the things you want to do and experiencing what you want to experience, the fuller and richer life you'll have. We have all been afraid, but if we avoid experiencing the negative, we vastly reduce the possibilities of life.

Difficulties in life strengthen the mind and expand our views on the horizon of the potential. We should be taking risks and working hard while we can, reading and exercising, enjoying time with friends and family, and finding out more about ourselves.

Take a moment and consider what things in life make you feel alive. Do you do enough of these things? Don't worry about the past or the future, focus on what you can do in the present and strive to achieve the Stoic's idea of "optimal living."

People without purpose in life are as good as dead, so find your light. Don't get too comfortable just because it is easier and safer. Walk through life not worrying about outcomes, because those are things you can't control, but be mindful of your efforts and intentions, because those are very much under your control. The secret to having a great life lies in serenity, which comes with the knowledge that you have done your best.

> *"You are the one who knows yourself, of how much you are worth to yourself and for how much you are selling yourself... Consider at what price you sell your integrity; but please, for God's sake, don't sell it cheap."*
>
> — EPICTETUS

We all have certain roles in life, and how well we go through life depends on how well we balance these roles. There are three kinds of roles. First is our role as a human, a member of the human 'polis' (a city in ancient Greece but one in its ideal form for philosophical purposes). The Stoics introduced the term "cosmopolitan," meaning "citizen of the world" and explained that we are all in the same place and that we have to take care of that place.

Next, there are roles assigned to us based on circumstances, such as somebody's son or daughter, which we didn't choose. Finally, there are roles that we choose, such as our career, or being a parent.

The first role trumps every other role and we have to balance all three. This is done using two virtues: the practical wisdom of knowing what is and what isn't good for you, and temperance, the idea that you can balance your life by putting the right amount of energy into the things you do.

Imagine you're an actor and you're playing a role that is not completely fleshed out. For example, people play the role of a mother in many different ways, but you play this role in the way you think is the right way to play it. The goal is not to reach perfection but to be the best version of yourself, or to be better than you were yesterday, one step at a time.

5

MINDSET AND PERSPECTIVE

As you can see, based on what we've learned so far, the great Stoic truth is that the universe was meant to be in harmony. It is rational, ordered and intelligent. We are all a part of the universe and we all have a role in building harmony. When we realize this, there is calm and tranquility, as we see and understand the flow of the world, and nothing shocks us as it used to. We can deal with our emotions and also accept what happens.

Stoicism is a very good guide to life that enables us to walk through life on the path of wisdom, determination, and self-control. It provides us with an invaluable apparatus to excel and be the best we can be. When we apply this philosophy to life, we see that it is based on reason and action, and teaches us the essential skills to prosper in any situation.

Although you can't establish the order of the outer world, you have been given a small locus of control to generate the order of your internal world. You can control how you respond to the world: your perceptions, desires, beliefs, and motivations. But we all have weaknesses, so one way to control them, as Epictetus suggests, is to counterattack the character flaws with the opposite habits.

If it is fear of pain, train yourself not to be afraid. Maybe you really enjoy the physical pleasure you derive from eating, so try to fast. Every change we want to make is a process, and it begins with our minds.

PART 1: NATURE

> *"Let us keep to the way which Nature has mapped out for us and let us not swerve therefrom. If we follow Nature, all is easy and unobstructed; but if we combat Nature, our life differs not a whit from that of men who row against the current."*
>
> — *SENECA*

Being in harmony with the world means being in harmony with your own nature. Not the beastly part that is led by our basic needs, but the part with the ability of higher thinking and reasoning. These abilities have not been given to us without cause, so use them. We perceive the world through our senses, and in the end, we decide if something is true or false and what its value is.

> *"For good or for ill, life and nature are governed by laws that we can't change. The quicker we accept this, the more tranquil we can be."*
>
> — *EPICTETUS*

In all matters of life, no matter how small or grand, act in the agreement of nature. When you eat, sleep, work or relax, do it mindfully in harmony with nature. When we practice the principles of Stoic philosophy in everyday tasks, inner peace follows and remains even in difficult situations.

Emotion

Can we believe in our feelings?

People are often said to be rational beings, but in reality, we are also very emotional beings. Often history has been the stage of horrific acts committed by human beings with passion. Beyond these large-scale dramas, our daily lives are plagued by instances where proper behavior is sacrificed in favor of ego and instinct.

In theatrical tragedies, such as Shakespeare's *King Lear* or *Romeo and Juliet*, acts aroused by passion have led to an unfortunate chain of events, betrayal and death.

This is the fate of the characters of the great tragedies, but how many times have our little everyday dramas evolved in a negative direction because of our lack of control over ourselves? How many times have our passionate actions led us to the edge of the abyss?

For the purpose of mastering our emotions, the Stoics recommend that we first observe and understand them, and then break them down by recognizing their true nature. In their works, we find an astonishing analysis of various emotions and their causes.

> *"It never ceases to amaze me: we all love ourselves more than other people, but care more about their opinion than our own."*
>
> — *MARCUS AURELIUS*

Other people or things themselves cannot hurt us, but how we perceive them is a different matter. We need to remind ourselves that we cannot choose the external circumstances: does someone love us, will the person hire us, when will the person disappear from our life? But we can choose our response to them. We all deserve to be the best version of ourselves, for ourselves, not for or because of others.

> *"Choose not to be harmed - and you won't feel harmed. Don't feel harmed - and you haven't been."*
>
> — *MARCUS AURELIUS*

People don't have the power to hurt you, it is you who gives them that power. It is always your choice to see things as hurtful. Pull back from the situation and don't let the moment ignite your emotions. It all comes down to the way we perceive a thing, so if we don't deal with the emotion and accept it, it can grow in our imagination and become a hindrance, whether it is positive or negative. Too much of anything can act as a poison.

> *"We are more often frightened than hurt, and we suffer more in imagination than in reality."*
>
> — *SENECA*

The Happiness Triangle

The Stoic Happiness Triangle is a visual representation of the core of Stoic philosophy. Inside the triangle is eudaimonia and surrounding it are three principles: 1) Live with

Areté, 2) Focus on what we can control and 3) Take responsibility.

Eudaimonia can only be found within and you do so by practicing the three principles. The first principle is to live with Areté. The term "Arete" is directly translated as "virtue," "excellence" or "expressing the best version of oneself." We need to express our best self if we want to reach eudaimonia and live a happy life.

> *"An emerald shines even if it's worth is not spoken of."*
>
> — MARCUS AURELIUS

The best way to explain Areté is to say that it is the highest quality that can be attained. So, to live with Areté is to focus on the quality of every action and experience.

> *"In your actions, don't procrastinate. In your conversations, don't confuse. In your thoughts, don't wander. In your soul, don't be passive or aggressive. In your life, don't be all about business."*
>
> — MARCUS AURELIUS

Areté is also described as a moral virtue, and it challenges us to express ourselves in accord with the good life, to avoid excess and defect. It teaches us to carry ourselves with courage, wisdom, and discipline.

The second principle of focusing on what we can control is the most discussed in the philosophy of Stoicism.

> *"You can be happy if you know this secret: some things are within your power to control, and some things are not."*
>
> — EPICTETUS

The single most important practice in Stoicism is noticing the difference between things we can or cannot control. We can get to the state of eudaimonia if we can focus our efforts and time on the things over which we have control and accept the rest as it is.

You will not only be happier, but you'll save your energy - emotional and physical - and you'll have an advantage over others who are fighting a battle that is already lost. Focus on things you can control.

The third and final principle of happiness is to take responsibility. You must take personal responsibility, no one is coming to save you. You and only you are responsible for your life.

> *"Waste no more time arguing what a good man should be. Be one."*
>
> — MARCUS AURELIUS

When we take responsibility and focus on the things we can control, we discover how powerful we really are. We cannot change the weather, others' behavior or the situation, but we can change ourselves and how we respond. Take the initiative and decide what your life is about, express your best self and strive to reach eudaimonia.

Love

> *"If you wish to be loved, love."*
>
> — SENECA

Stoics love deeply and without shame, and accept love as something only deepest wisdom can comprehend. But they also apply their core beliefs, meaning they don't allow the emotion of love to overpower them.

> *"Unhappy men, who are the slave even of a girl... Why then do you still call yourself free?"*
>
> — EPICTETUS

Epictetus considered passion and lust to be excessive impulses connected to the animal side of human nature. He believed that if you become a slave to love, it is not love. Only the wise are capable of truly loving, as they can distinguish between truth and illusion.

> *"If someone is incapable of distinguishing good things from bad and neutral things from either - well, how could such a person be capable of love? The power to love, then, belongs only to the wise man."*
>
> — EPICTETUS

Love - Family - Siblings

> *"Adapt yourself to the life you have been given, and truly love the people with whom destiny has surrounded you."*

— *MARCUS AURELIUS*

We are not isolated entities, but rather essential parts of the universe. The Stoics speak about how one should interact with other people, but the question of the family tends to be neglected.

But we can explain the Stoic approach as role ethics, in which we recognize our natural relation to one another. We play a variety of roles in our lives and a contented life comes from balancing these roles to the best of our ability, whether as family, friend, colleague or citizen. Once we know who we are and with whom we are connected, we know how to behave.

For example, let's consider our relationship to our father. We naturally feel obligated to take care of him, respect him and listen to his advice. The nature of his character, whether good or bad, is secondary. We can't control who our family is, so this man, even if we don't find him acceptable, is our father.

> *"It is silly to try to escape other people's faults. They are inescapable. Just try to escape your own."*
>
> — *MARCUS AURELIUS*

Suppose you have a sibling who doesn't treat you well. According to Stoicism, their treatment of you shouldn't make a difference in how you relate to them. Instead, focus on your purpose, which is your road to freedom and eudaimonia.

Actions of others are not in your control and therefore you shouldn't concern yourself with them. When you are engaging in wise and decent acts, you will not feel victimized by others. Other people cannot hurt you without your consent; this is something over which only you have control.

While others' words have no power over us, obviously physical abuse does. But Stoics preach the training of the body as well as the mind, so we can choose and control how we respond to those who may try to physically harm us.

Parents, Elders, and Children

The structure of the Ancient Roman family was based on the nuclear family structure and on the hierarchy. Extended family could be included, in which case they would use the term "familia" to describe a family.

The oldest male in the family was the "paterfamilias," or the head of the house, and had absolute authority over everyone in the household. If this figure, which was usually the father, grandfather, or uncle, had living sons, they and their children would also be under his authority.

Stoic philosopher Hierocles described the Stoic concept of cosmopolitanism—the idea that all human beings are part of a single community—through the use of concentric circles. He described individuals as consisting of a series of circles: The first circle is the human mind, the second is immediate family, the third, extended family, then the local community. The next circle is the neighboring towns, then the country, and finally the entire human race. One additional circle was added later by comtemporary Stoics to represent a Stoic's duty of care to the environment and all living beings on Earth.

Hierocles' model breaks the standard hierarchical structure of family, in accordance with Stoic philosophy. The father is placed in the same circle as the mother and the rest of the nuclear family. Additionally, the parents are believed to be the ethical role models, not just authoritarian figures.

Love – Relationships

> *"If you long for your son or your friend [or your partner] when it is not given you to have him, know that you are longing for a fig in the winter time."*
>
> — *EPICTETUS*

As with everything else, the Stoics differentiated between the good and bad in love, just as we do today. We know there are differences between terms like attraction, desire, love, lust, passion, devotion, and yearning.

Love we often give freely without needing anything in return. The quality of our love does not depend on outside factors, but lust, on the other hand, means we desire something which is not in our control.

When we are lustful, we crave the body of another human being, and if we cannot satisfy this desire, we suffer. Epictetus described the things that are not in our control as "weak, slavish, restrained, belonging to others."

Today the romantic love ideal has become such an important pursuit that we have elevated it to our ultimate concern. We put it on a pedestal, above culture, spirituality, and religion. Some of us make love the center of our life's pursuit. The problem with this is that it doesn't last. When two people fall in love, they experience a period often called the "honeymoon phase," but

after the euphoria wanes, we may begin to feel cheated. Without the rose-colored glasses, we start seeing the other as a flawed human being, and may then seek romantic interest elsewhere because this one doesn't feel right anymore.

> *"He who fails to obtain the object of his desire is disappointed, and he who incurs the object of his aversion is wretched."*
>
> — EPICTETUS

The resulting jealousy often leads to possessiveness, and a need to control the other person, to assure ourselves that they don't do things we don't want them to do. These kinds of relationships are neither healthy nor do they lead to inner peace. The Stoics didn't disapprove of relationships, but they also didn't recommend clinging or lust. Seneca found indulgence in lust to be one of the worst sins.

> *"... among the worst cases I count also those who give their time to nothing but drink and lust; for these are the most shameful preoccupations of them all."*
>
> — SENECA

Beyond indulging in lust, however, Seneca respected love and meaningful relationships between people. In fact, he valued marriage and all the duties involved, and condemned adultery and divorce. Such a stance is congruent with Stoic ethics that point to living a virtuous life above everything else.

Ultimately, the people we love are not in our control and we can lose them in a heartbeat. And although Stoics value virtue above all else, that doesn't mean that intimate relationships and virtue contradict each other. Even lust can be part of a virtuous life, as long as it is not overindulged.

Friendship

"Nothing, however, delights the mind as much as loving and loyal friendship."

— SENECA

We often speak of good friends, usually when that person has been of help to us. The Stoics certainly see that friendship has to be helpful on both sides, but the value of friendship for Stoics goes much deeper. Stoics consider their friends good because of their character, virtues, and understanding of nature in such a way that they admire them.

We value friendship through shared experiences, respect for one another and common interests. If you choose a friend as a Stoic, you will choose a friend based on their quality as a human being.

When describing a friend, we may mention how long we've been friends, what we've gone through together, how we met and how well we know each other. But this friendship may lack the quality of a good friendship, according to Stoics.

How can we choose our friends today, when we are not as virtuous as the Stoic philosophers of old? We choose people as friends based on similarity to ourselves, and people we perceive as being of the same quality as us. But can we learn anything new from such a person? This is one of the things we can control: what type of people we surround ourselves with.

> *"The key is to keep company only with people who uplift you, whose presence calls forth your best."*
>
> — EPICTETUS

The Stoic friend is a friend who "... treats their friends exactly as they treat themselves," as Marcus Aurelius would say. Don't hesitate to act on your generous impulse, especially if a friend needs you. As long as you take your reason with you, you will be safe and it is our duty in our friendships to help one another.

These friendships are relationships of mutual help, in a sense that they have shared beliefs and affection, and they are friendships that possess wisdom and mutual understanding.

Virtue

When we described the Happiness Triangle earlier, we introduced the term "Areté," or virtue, and talked about living with Areté as a means to reach eudaimonia, or a happy state of life. The Stoics talked about four main virtues and grouped all other virtues into these four.

These four virtues according to Stoic philosophy are prudence, or wisdom, justice, or morality, fortitude, or courage, and temperance, or moderation.

Prudence, as the opposite of ignorance, is most important because it refers to the understanding of what is good or bad in life. Justice is about being moral, as in doing the things that are just, or right. Temperance refers to moderation, or self-control; in other words, not indulging in things. It is the mindful approach to everything we do that teaches us that we can enjoy everything in moderation. Fortitude is a simpler virtue, as it means courage. Courage refers to fighting and mastering fears and looking at things the way they are rather than how we want them to be.

Even the perfect sage need to practice self-mastery of these virtues daily.

Self-love

If you love yourself, you will most certainly do what is best for you. The only relationship that we have control over is the one with ourselves. This relationship is a draft for all external relationships. If someone is acting in a hateful manner towards themselves, that is how they are teaching themselves to interact with others.

Self-confidence

> *"If you want any good then get it from within."*
>
> — *EPICTETUS*

Stoicism doesn't really deal with self-confidence, because confidence naturally follows from practicing Stoicism on the path to serenity. With inner peace comes self-confidence. Forget about perfection, just be sure you are doing the best you can. True confidence comes from doing the best we can and not worrying about the outcome, since we can't control it.

Self-ambition

"A man's worth is no greater than the worth of his ambition."

— MARCUS AURELIUS

Many practitioners of Stoic philosophy were famous soldiers, leaders, writers, and artists. Marcus Aurelius, for example, was an emperor, so it's hard to believe he wasn't ambitious. But Stoics take satisfaction from wanting and being good at their craft, so their ambition is to be highly skilled.

Ambition and effort cannot be drawn from the external but are instead tied to our own actions and thoughts.

Self-determination

Determination, or willpower, is one of the greatest human characteristics. When we lose our determination, it can lead us to lose self-control and, as a result, make bad decisions.

If we are tired in the morning and choose not to get up, we may lose the willpower to do the things we need to do. Self-determination should be a habit, so we're able to make ourselves go the extra mile even when we are tired.

Giving and receiving

Our universal nature is what makes us feel for each other and every living being. We like to help others and we feel this is the right thing to do. But do we help because it makes us feel good or out of true unselfishness? We must be mindful that the reason we help others isn't because of the good feeling we get from it, but because it is the right course of action.

Helping others too much is a form of indulgence and it is easy to lose our path if helping others becomes our main priority. With giving comes receiving, as the things we give out to the world will come back to us, though perhaps in a different form.

Desire

Desires seek and demand to be fulfilled, and if we don't get what we want we are devastated. It is natural for us to avoid things we find undesirable, especially inevitable things like death or sickness, but this can cause us and others greater suffering.

Stoicism helps us understand that desire and aversion are habits that can be changed. It teaches us to restrain our aversion to things outside of our control and to instead steer our efforts toward things we can control.

Desire is not in our control, because it tends to be the wishing for something we can't control, so disappointment often follows.

Wealth and abundance

> *"For the wise man does not consider himself unworthy of any gifts from Fortune's hands: he does not love wealth but he would rather have it; he does not admit into his heart but into his home; and what wealth is his he does not reject but keeps, wishing it to supply greater scope for him to practice his virtue."*
>
> — SENECA

Seneca is advising us to not be a slave to our wealth but rather the master of it. We need to constantly question whether we're afraid to lose it, because if we are, this means that our wealth has become our master. The irony in having material wealth is the desire to have more of it, which is another form of indulgence upon which Stoics frown. Moderation is key.

> *"The only wealth which you will keep forever is the wealth you have given away."*
>
> — MARCUS AURELIUS

Marcus Aurelius held a public sale of his imperial belongings so he could fund his expedition against Germanic tribes, who were pillaging, killing people and raping women. After his reign ended, he left Rome with a replenished treasury and the Germanic tribes were suppressed. He was able to do this because he thought of happiness as a choice, not a circumstance. He found his happiness in virtue, not pleasure, as did most Romans of the time, and this empowered him.

The trouble with our modern times is that people aren't willing to give up pleasure for virtue.

"What we do now echoes in eternity."

— MARCUS AURELIUS

PART II: DEPRESSION

I think it's safe to say that everyone encounters depression at some point in their life, at least to some degree. The Stoic way to conquer depression lies in their dichotomy of control. It is futile to worry about that which you can't control. Whenever you start sensing these kinds of emotions creeping up on you, try to slow your thought process. Breathe and think things through logically, so you can make the distinction between the facts and your impression. Ask yourself, is the real cause of your depression the outside world or is it your expectations of it?

We must deliberately choose to control our words, thoughts, emotions, and actions. At first, it will be hard to change your mental attitude and take control of your mind, especially over emotions. But by doing and practicing these things every day, you will wake up one morning and choose how you want to feel. Increase your awareness of your thoughts and emotions, and your perspective of the external world will change.

Take control of your words, because these are easy to control. Decide that you will never use a word of defeat, speak ill of others or yourself or pass around negative judgment. Take a step back, calm your thoughts and choose not to speak in the voice of depression.

Take control of your actions to improve your health and control your emotions and thoughts. Sometimes a health problem is the cause of depression. Sunlight, water, and fresh air can all counteract the feelings of depresssion. Even the way we move has a tremendous effect on our mind. Try walking through the world standing straight and tall, and you will feel more powerful.

Anxiety

The philosophy of Stoicism teaches us to focus on the now because what we do in the now is the only thing we can control. The outcome of any decision is out of our control, so all we can do is to make the best decision we can.

> *"For truth has its own definite boundaries, but that which arises from uncertainty is delivered over to guesswork and the irresponsible license of a frightened mind. That is why no fear is so ruinous and so uncontrollable as panic fear. For other fears are groundless, but this fear is witless."*
>
> — SENECA

The feeling of anxiety is a formed habit, so train yourself to live without it. Once you start practicing the Stoic view, this will become a new habit and you will find yourself calmer. Anxiety is grounded in the worry about what might happen, but once we realize that whatever happens is not in our control, we find peace of mind.

Hate and anger

What good has hate and anger brought to anyone? These are merely a waste of emotional energy. Don't burden your soul and mind with such petty feelings.

> *"How much more grievous are the consequences of anger, than the causes of it."*
>
> — MARCUS AURELIUS

When we are led by anger, we make decisions or say things that make us feel bad afterward. This happens to all of us. But according to Stoicism, when we feel anger, it shows us how unrealistic our expectations were of the world and that we incorrectly gave control over to the external.

Anger is merely a battle with ourselves and we can defeat it because we control the emotion, it does not control us.

Sometimes we find ourselves hating others and sometimes others hate us. In the first case, we have wrongly given power to external circumstances to dictate our feelings. In the second instance, we might find out that someone hates us and it might even come as a surprise, but there is no need to place value on what others think, because that is out of your control and only you truly know yourself.

> *"The best revenge is not to be like your enemy."*
>
> — MARCUS AURELIUS

To spend your time on an act of revenge when you can actually do something productive, to Stoics means to dwell in the past. When we cling to past feelings, it affects us in the present, as well as the future.

Of course, passivity isn't a Stoic principle, so if an enemy attacks you, do what is in accordance with nature, which is to defend yourself the best way you can. When you have control over yourself, no enemy can bring you down.

Judgment

> *"Impressions, striking a person's mind as soon as he perceives something within the range of his senses, are not voluntary or subject to his will, they impose themselves on people's attention almost with a will of their own. But the act of assent which endorses these impressions is voluntary and a function of the human will."*
>
> — EPICTETUS

Making judgments, both consciously and subconsciously, is a characteristic of being human. We compare ourselves to other people, we see someone and make a judgment about what kind of a person they are based on their appearance, voice, manner, social status, etc.

> *"You always own the option of having no opinion. There is never any need to get worked up or to trouble your soul about things you can't control. These things are not asking to be judged by you. Leave them alone."*
>
> — MARCUS AURELIUS

We cannot control other people or their actions and opinions, but we can control ourselves. Mastery of the self is the basic principle here. There is no need to be annoyed by another's appearance, or the way they speak or behave. Accept them as they are; they are not in your control. We are all different. What works for them may not work for you and vice versa.

Being jealous and envious is no way to live. It draws focus away from important things. These emotions are not enjoyable or fulfilling, and they are purposeless, but we still succumb to them. But they are blinding us to possibilities. While we are desiring the life of somebody else, we are not seeing the way we can better our own life or even acknowledging the good in it. We lose the ability to enjoy the things we already have or to make them better.

Don't excuse these emotions as fuel or stimuli for improving your life. You don't really want your life to be exactly like the life of someone else. You need to find your own path, and what is best for you.

Adversity

"Fire is the test of gold; adversity, of strong men."

— SENECA

When we are facing adversity, we should behave as if it is an opportunity, not something to be feared. Find a way to turn obstacles into opportunities and grow through them. If you regularly look into the face of adversity, it won't catch you by surprise, you will find a way to deal with it.

"You are unfortunate in my judgment, for you have never been unfortunate. You have passed through life with no antagonist to face you; no one will know what you were capable of, not even you yourself."

— SENECA

Through adversity, we learn what we are truly capable of and we discover new parts of ourselves and our minds. We become more and more successful in facing adversity by simply facing it each time it appears. This can help us appreciate all that is good in our lives as well as drive us to continually make life better.

Courage and bravery

The bravery to take action and to see things as they are is the Stoic philosophy. We show our character through our actions, through facing our fears and dealing with things in a calm manner. Those who have the courage to face adversity can make the most out of the present moment, without worrying about the future, because having the courage to make today better is the way to build a better future.

Do you want to lose weight? Have the courage to take action, even if the results aren't visible right away. Have the courage to stick with your work-out and meal plan. Give yourself time to see progress. Set a goal of running a marathon one year from now and stick with it.

Maybe there is someone you like but haven't gotten close to. Be brave and go and talk to them, tell them how you feel. Don't worry about the outcome - it is not in your control, but your actions are. If you don't try, you will never know what might have been.

You want to finish school? Remove distractions; have the courage to say no to your friends when they ask you out. What is more important, passing an exam or sitting in a coffee shop and gossiping?

Decide what goal you are pursuing and bravely give it your very best.

Self-control and self-discipline

The biggest motivation for self-discipline is to have a reason to do something. Self-discipline starts with finding your purpose, and then nothing can stop you from achieving your goal. Your own will is always within your control.

I believe we all have a purpose, something that we were created to do. It is our duty to find and carry out that purpose because that is what gets us out of bed in the morning and what makes us feel alive. This feeling of having a purpose is what will keep you moving forward even when you're exhausted or lack motivation.

Self-discipline will ensure that you see your goal through to the end. Build a practical plan of action that will enable you to accomplish your goal. Commit to all actions, even the smallest ones, as long as they keep you focused on reaching your goal.

The Stoics talk about self-control on a regular basis. Mastering self-control will keep you away from addictive behaviors, or from acting on impulse and will keep you focused on the things that matter.

Having self-control ensures that we will not be easily enslaved by external forces that are out of our control. We are not meant to spend our lives eating, drinking and sleeping to excess. There are many ways to practice self-control, such as fasting, restricting usage of our phones or at least of social media, chewing food slowly to better enjoy it, reducing a smoking or drinking habit, and so on.

It takes some effort, but self-control can lead us to a better, more fulfilled life, where we're not slaves to destructive habits.

PART III: HOBBIES AND INTERESTS

Stoic philosophy involves taking on a challenge, enduring it, learning from that experience and applying that newfound wisdom to life. Hobbies and interests are no different. We all have something we enjoy doing and which makes us feel relaxed, but in this hectic world, we often don't allow time for these activities. The Stoics valued the activities that kept them centered and healthy. They took care of their bodies as well as their minds.

Sometimes we find it hard to commit to our interests and hobbies long enough to see their potential or learn from them. Challenge yourself. Maybe you want to learn to knit. When someone else does it, it seems so effortless, but when you actually have the needle in your hand, it isn't so effortless. But overcoming that first obstacle and sticking with it, proving that it *is* something you can do, is very rewarding. And in the end, you have a unique scarf of your own making! Then you can move on to hats and sweaters.

It is like that with everything we do in life. Our hobbies and interest provide us with the initial spark, but there is a bit of a Stoic in all of us when we decide to stay with something.

Everything you do, do with effort and commitment. Stoics are always in search of excellence, so pursue your best in all the things you do. Even if you spend little time on your interests, strive to give your best.

Work

Work is a broad term in Stoicism. Today work is what makes our life possible; we need the money from our work to buy food, clothes, and housing. But how would a Stoic perform their duties in life?

"You must plan your life, one action at a time."

— MARCUS AURELIUS

We must focus our efforts on the task at hand. When we focus on what is in our control and treat adversity as a challenge rather than an obstacle, we have power over our productivity.

This is practical advice from Stoics. It provides us with an objective-oriented rule to follow. Don't let yourself become distracted or disturbed, and simply finish the task at hand. There are many benefits to this way of thinking: you finish your job quickly, your boss is pleased, you train your focus and self-control, and your success will make you feel even more motivated.

Stoic principles shape us into responsible, efficient people. In the workplace, the Stoic philosophy serves as a great work ethic. A Stoic is able to face adversity and rise to a challenge while still completing the task and leading by example. A Stoic will always apply reason to achieve the best outcome.

On the other hand, you won't find a Stoic workaholic, because they believe in balance. After all, work is not the sole purpose of life - there is so much more that makes life worth living. In addition to our professional life, we have family life, social life, hobbies and leisure time. The challenge is to balance all of these, especially today when the world moves so fast.

To a Stoic, life without harmony and compromise among the different roles we play is impossible. We cannot give one hundred percent to every aspect of our life. Stoicism is about acknowledging the complexity and diversity of life.

The Stoic philosophy sees life as a long-term project. This 'whole life' perspective and decisions based on the truth consciously lead to a chosen set of values. Indulgence of one thing and avoidance of others is not a Stoic life, as it lacks harmony. Someone who is expert at their job, but who neglects their family is not living a balanced Stoic existence.

Stoicism is most focused on self-improvement. To work on oneself is the most important task in Stoicism, so this is an ideal philosophy for self-care and perseverance. But it is also about hard work, with no shortcuts or assistance.

The path of a Stoic life is indeed difficult, but it is also very rewarding. It involves constant work, but without it, much like athletes and their training, the muscles of our mind would deflate. We must push ourselves to remain sharp and agile. The more we push ourselves forward, the better we become. There is always something to learn and even if we cannot learn it all, we cannot stop working on our self-improvement.

How time should be spent

If we want to live well, we have to be constant students of the greatest teacher, life. We cannot turn back time and we cannot prolong our life. Time is precious and the amount we have of it is limited.

So many of us waste valuable time waiting for life to happen to us, instead of living in the now. We think happiness lies in the future and is simply waiting us. But our future is not in our control. The life we are waiting for or striving toward by spending so much time at work might never happen. We become so worried about the future that we allow time to rush past us unobserved. Don't let yourself regret not making the most of life.

Seneca compares time to a rushing stream that won't always flow. If you were lost in the desert and stumbled across a stream of water, wouldn't you rush to drink as much as you could in fear it would disappear? That is how we should use our time, making the most of it in the present.

Your years ahead are worth planning for, but don't let them take away today. You can only live one moment at a time. Live life for yourself, don't just exist. We all have things we want to do in life, but most of us don't actually do them. We do what's convenient, work the job we don't like to pay the bills, or pretend to love someone because we want a family.

We fool ourselves that one day things will be better and that we don't have time for new goals. Being busy with things we don't enjoy is the greatest distraction from living. The best time investment is the one you invest in creating a life you love living.

> *"While wasting our time hesitating and procrastinating, life goes on."*
>
> — SENECA

To bolster our defenses against the spectre of an uncertain future, the Stoics used a form of negative visualization called *premeditatio malorum*. This is an exercise in which we imagine what could go wrong or be taken away, in other words, negative outcomes. This tactic helps prepare us in the event of a negative outcome and removes the sting of surprise. It also builds resilience when we realize we have the fortitude to weather whatever comes in the future, good or bad.

6

BUSINESS STOICS

This chapter takes us out of the waters of theoretical philosophy and brings us back to practice. In this chapter, we'll discuss how Stoicism can help you attain a better position in your workplace, get that promotion you've been hoping for, or even start your own business.

Just because Stoics live in relative simplicity, and only work toward the pursuit of virtue, doesn't mean they live in caves. In fact, some of the world's richest men embody the Stoic philosophy quite well… and this is no accident.

STOICISM AND ENTREPRENEURSHIP

Zeno of Citium, the founder of Stoicism, was once himself an entrepreneur. He was quite successful as he engaged in trade, and as his voyages grew more and more frequent, his profits became larger and larger.

While most entrepreneurs might only expect a metaphorical shipwreck to follow such positive events, Zeno was faced with a literal one. He lost everything he was carrying, and barely made it to Athens. Within a few years, he had not only rebuilt his wealth, but founded the philosophy of Stoicism. He would later say:

> "I made a prosperous voyage when I suffered shipwreck."

Now, what would the modern-day equivalent of this be? Let's say you've launched a new tech startup, and you're trying to acquire more customers. You succeed! You're starting to rake in the profits, and you're reinvesting everything in the business.

Business is booming, but suddenly you're faced with a competitor who is backed by Google. Their superior service, funded by billions of dollars, outshines and outpaces anything you've been able to do, and ultimately your business is ruined and you're left with nothing.

Who could fault someone for despairing after such an event? A Stoic would, because to sink into despair isn't acceptable. Many of us might simply give up on our dream, but a Stoic would accept the fact that the competitor was an external force outside of their control. Then they would find ways to use this painful event as a driving force for action.

For example, in the above case, the appearance of the competitor means that your ideas are so good that even Google wants a piece of the pie. Rather than letting themselves be trapped by negative thoughts, a Stoic would burst out like a butterfly from a cocoon, becoming even stronger.

Now, let's not be as dramatic (after all, few of us will go as far as competing with Google in our pursuits). Instead, let's suppose a regular entrepreneur is trying to make money by playing the stock market. This may sound odd, but the stock market is where the Stoic philosophy shines brightest. It is a world out of our control, like gambling.

A Stoic would look at all their investments rationally rather than emotionally, and would under- stand whether or not they've made the right calls. A common pitfall that traders fall into is acting rashly after they've made a profitable trade. A Stoic would not behave like this, saving themselves from potential losses.

Furthermore, a Stoic attitude gives confidence. Once you've become at peace with things outside of your control, you subconsciously begin giving off the air of a confident person. This has shown itself to be an integral aspect of successful investing.

Stoicism also shows us the most profitable way to treat workers. Many companies err on the side of caution and either underpay or overpay their workers. A Stoic would merely ask themselves, "How can I optimize our work efficiency?" They would consult scientific literature and seek expert advice, then choose the best way to pay their workers so everyone is satisfied.

After all, an unhappy worker is usually an unproductive worker.

While growing your business, you will be faced with many stressful challenges and situations. In fact, this is so common that burnout is practically a staple of startup businesses. But Stoics are immune to such burnout. All of those stressors that plague the regular entrepreneur will not phase the Stoic. Their reaction is merely, "This too shall pass," before they continue on with their work. In some cases, stressful events even serve as motivation to work harder. This is a trait that is extremely valuable to investors, which is evident from the abundance of Stoic trait-exhibiting people on the world's richest list.

It isn't an exaggeration to say that behind every successful entrepreneur there is at least a little bit of a Stoic mindset. After all, bouncing back from hardships is about 50 percent of what makes a successful entrepreneur.

Another way in which Stoicism is tailored to entrepreneurs is the way it promotes innovation and contradicting habit.

> *"So in the majority of other things, we address circumstances not in accordance with the right assumptions, but mostly by following wretched habit. Since all that I've said is the case, the person in training must seek to rise above, so as to stop seeking out pleasure and steering away from pain; to stop clinging to living and abhorring death; and in the case of property and money, to stop valuing receiving over giving."*
>
> — MUSONIUS RUFUS

In our modern day, this can be seen as entrepreneurs challenging "the way [a particular thing] has always been done." So much is done a certain way out of tradition, rather than being based on a concrete, rational reason. The traditional, habit-based mindset is not the mindset of an entrepreneur, it is the mindset of a worker who has given up on ever moving upward.

Unfortunately, what happens to many entrepreneurs, even successful ones, is that they forget about themselves. As much as the startup is vital to you, you are vital to the startup. This means you need to treat yourself much like a startup, or in the words of a man much wiser than I:

> "But what does Socrates say? 'Just as one person delights in improving his farm, and another his horse, so I delight in attending to my own improvement day by day."
>
> — EPICTETUS

Do not forget about your own self-improvement. Even if your startup is taking much of your time, go to the gym, read books, improve yourself! In the end, you are the most powerful asset of your startup.

STOICISM AND MOVING UP IN THE WORKPLACE

Beyond entrepreneurship, let's examine the principles of Stoicism as they pertain to traditional employment.

After all, most of us are not cut out to be entrepreneurs, but maybe the life of an executive of a fortune-500 company is more appealing. So, how can Stoicism help us in the average workplace?

Stoicism helps us remember that we need to prioritize ourselves. Maybe you've noticed that at many companies, there are a few people who eat, live, and breathe their work. Weirdly enough, these people rarely get promoted. This is because companies want to see initiative and drive for something beyond oneself. If they feel like you're an integral part of their operation and don't want to lose you, they'll want to promote you. Those who show themselves to be extremely capable, but make no secret about the fact that if another company offered better terms, they would jump ship, are more likely to be promoted.

It can be very easy to forget your own value in the workplace, but remember - the company hired you for a reason. So, keep working on yourself. If your current company doesn't recognize the improvements you've made, and isn't willing to offer you what you're worth, do the rational thing and find another job. Stoicism helps us shed outdated attachments like "company loyalty" and similar irrational beliefs.

The confidence that Stoicism gives you can help you secure a promotion at an existing job but it can also help you find a new position. Interviewers and hiring managers respect and admire confidence, and want to see this trait in their employees. They want to see someone who sits up straight and looks them in the eye. Someone who will speak clearly and take responsibility, not someone who will stutter and shift blame.

Consider your last job. What was the largest source of stress in it? It was probably your coworkers, right? Office politics are a tedious, and often stressful element of many workplaces.

But with a Stoic mindset, we can ignore the behavior of our colleagues, and even bosses we dislike. We have no control over what they do or how they behave, so why let it bother us?

Simple changes to our thought processes like this one can illustrate the impact that Stoicism can have on our life and career. Additionally, the Stoic's resistance to habit makes you more likely to innovate in the workplace, try new things, and automate processes.

Bosses like workers who save them money, so if you manage to implement a useful innovation, you'll be looking at a promotion pretty soon!

STOICISM AND THE RICH

As we've noted several times, many of the world's richest people follow some of the principles of Stoicism, but let's elaborate on that a bit here.

The primary things you need to become rich are similar to the principles of Stoicism. First of all, you need the ability to look past emotions and rationally assess risk and reward. Most wealthy people have grown their riches either by investing or being entrepreneurs, and in both cases, being able to evaluate risk without emotional attachment is an extremely important skill.

The next skill you need is the ability to use your failures as learning opportunities. If you despair every time you fail, rather than learn from your failure, you'll never increase your wealth. After all, your time is finite, and time spent moping is time wasted. Accept your failures and move on, even if they were your fault.

Philanthropy is another element of being wealthy, but donations made by the rich tend to be much more calculated and thought-out than those made by average people. Let's consider the Bill & Melinda Gates Foundation, for example. The Gates' work to save children from poverty and disease, but not simply because they feel compassion and helping these children makes them feel good.

They help because they understand that these children will now grow up healthy and will contribute to a better society and a better world. This rational, planned approach to philanthropy is quite Stoic in nature, because it is driven by reason rather than solely by emotion.

The Stoic philosophy also attracts the rich and powerful because it is based on action rather than on thought and intent. Stoicism is wholly rooted in the pursuit of wisdom and virtue through action.

This active nature of Stoicism is necessary for keeping up with today's fast-paced world. Whether or not the rich and powerful among us know about Stoicism, the fact is that many Stoic principles are a necessary component of success.

7

WHAT OTHERS THINK OF STOICISM

Despite all we've learned so far, it's not all sunshine and rainbows. Stoicism isn't perfect, especially when put into practice, and in this chapter, we'll focus on the struggles one might have while attaining a Stoic mindset. After all, it's easy to talk about accepting grief, but a whole other thing to actually do it.

Furthermore, there are many other philosophies out there, and many of them have critiques of Stoicism, some of which are positive, and some of which aren't quite so. In this chapter, I've tried to present them as objectively as possible, while also responding to their criticisms to the best of my ability.

Finally, we'll talk about how it has worked out for me. I'll share my own, step-by-step journey of accepting a Stoic mindset. I would love to tell you that it was easy, and all it took was reading two or three texts for me to become a full-blown Stoic. Unfortunately, reality is rarely that kind, especially when the changes made are drastic. In fact, I'm still nowhere close to the ideal Stoic.

I am still sometimes driven by emotion, sometimes I fall into a rut and it takes me a while to climb out of it, and sometimes I get nervous. Stoicism hasn't made me perfect, but I'm convinced it has made me better.

THE CRITICISMS OF STOICISM

First, let's tackle an easy criticism: Stoicism argues that people should repress their emotions, but scientific research has shown that this is detrimental to mental health, hence Stoicism is detrimental to mental health.

But this criticism stems not from objective reasoning, but rather from a misunderstanding of Stoicism. The Stoic doctrine doesn't say that we need to repress our emotions. Rather, it says that we should realize that external factors cannot be bad, and hence there will eventually be no reason for those negative emotions to arise in the first place. If these emotions are already there, Stoicism teaches us to accept them, and use them as motivation. Both of these things are very different from repressing.

Stoicism also doesn't have a problem with most positive emotions. Since emotions like joy don't lead us into flawed actions, Stoicism has nothing against it. Only emotions like fear or anger, which can actively impede our functioning as reasoning beings, are considered to be given rise from false judgments.

Accepting emotions is the act of understanding why you feel a certain way, and that you do feel that way. This is a level of self-understanding that has been demonstrated to help with mental health issues. The task is to simply accept them, not repress them, but keep them from impeding your function as a human being.

Alternatively, they can be used as motivation. I doubt anyone will say that a student who studies to spite the teacher who dislikes them is doing something unhealthy. While this isn't strictly Stoic (as it is done out of anger), it is an example of using emotions as motivation, rather than allowing them to constrain you.

Second, claiming that eudaimonia can be achieved entirely through pursuit of virtue has uncertain truth value. After all, a sage is not a common person, and it is almost impossible to verify whether someone has achieved eudaimonia. Epicureanism, for example, includes more factors than virtue in the achievement of eudaimonia.

Now, I'm not going to lie, this criticism has some legs to stand on. Proving that someone has reached eudaimonia is indeed impossible. After all, it is entirely an internal state. Until our MRI machines are advanced enough to be able to recognize such states of tranquility, I'm afraid we won't know if it's truly possible.

On the other hand, let's consider someone who has, most likely - at least according to popular belief - achieved it: Buddha. According to Buddhist religion, the Buddha became enlightened (reached eudaimonia) entirely through the pursuit of virtue and leaving the self behind. The Stoic and Buddhist philosophies are very similar, so if we agree that the Buddha achieved eudaimonia, then theoretically we would agree with Stoicism.

But let's assume for a second that the criticism is valid. To a certain degree I would even say it is. It is nearly impossible to obtain such mental control that things like physical torture or chemical drugs won't affect you. These externals fundamentally alter the biological makeup of the Stoic, and no matter their conviction, are bound to break them away from the enlightened state of eudaimonia.

Given this, I would argue that eudaimonia, being an ancient Greek invention (long before we knew about mind-altering drugs), excludes such extreme examples. Theoretically, though, I can imagine even physical torture being conquered. But yes, in the end I do agree that total eudaimonia is practically impossible.

But so what? Stoicism isn't about attaining virtue; at its core Stoicism is about the process of attaining virtue, rather than the final goal of reaching eudaimonia. While that is the final frontier of Stoicism, if you have not reached eudaimonia, you have not failed as a Stoic, for the very pursuit of it is considered virtuous.

The next criticism strikes at the very building blocks of Stoic philosophy: The way Stoic philosophy refers to nature is extremely vague and hard to justify. Is this "nature" the same nature we think of when we use the word in modern times? If that is the case, then it would be quite difficult to draw moral conclusions from it.

Alternatively, is it the divine nature, or *logos*, meaning "the active reason pervading and animating the Universe"? This works if you're a religious person, but it makes Stoicism rely on theism to exist. Does nature refer to an individual's ideal nature? Sure, that could work, but we aren't exactly certain what that means.

Personally, I think this is one of the more intriguing questions to think about. However, I believe the answer can be fairly simple because I think the issue from which this criticism stems is treating Stoicism as a religion.

Stoicism has no holy book and is an adaptable philosophy. It isn't an issue if the ancient Greeks had one idea for nature and we have a different one. If their idea doesn't work, then it is our duty as Stoics to update our philosophy.

A more clear-cut answer might be that Stoicism refers to the ideal nature of an individual, wherein is found altruism and reasonableness.

Finally, let us look at Nietzsche's lengthy criticism of Stoicism presented in his book *Beyond Good And Evil*.

> *"You desire to LIVE "according to Nature"? Oh, you noble Stoics, what fraud of words! Imagine to yourselves a being like Nature, boundlessly extravagant, boundlessly indifferent, without purpose or consideration, without pity or justice, at once fruitful and barren and uncertain: imagine to yourselves INDIFFERENCE as a power--how COULD you live in accordance with such indifference?*
>
> *"To live--is not that just endeavoring to be otherwise than this Nature? Is not living valuing, preferring, being unjust, being limited, endeavoring to be different? And granted that your imperative, "living according to Nature," means actually the same as "living according to life"--how could you do DIFFERENTLY? Why should you make a principle out of what you yourselves are, and must be?*
>
> *"In reality, however, it is quite otherwise with you: while you pretend to read with rapture the canon of your law in Nature,*

> *you want something quite the contrary, you extraordinary stage-players and self-deluders! In your pride you wish to dictate your morals and ideals to Nature, to Nature herself, and to incorporate them therein; you insist that it shall be Nature "according to the Stoa," and would like everything to be made after your own image, as a vast, eternal glorification and generalism of Stoicism! With all your love for truth, you have forced yourselves so long, so persistently, and with such hypnotic rigidity to see Nature FALSELY, that is to say, Stoically, that you are no longer able to see it otherwise--and to crown all, some unfathomable superciliousness gives you the Bedlamite hope that BECAUSE you are able to tyrannize over yourselves--Stoicism is self-tyranny--Nature will also allow herself to be tyrannized over: is not the Stoic a PART of Nature? . . .*
>
> *"But this is an old and everlasting story: what happened in old times with the Stoics still happens today, as soon as ever a philosophy begins to believe in itself. It always creates the world in its own image; it cannot do otherwise; philosophy is this tyrannical impulse itself, the most spiritual Will to Power, the will to "creation of the world," the will to the causa prima."*

This is quite a powerful critique (Nietzsche isn't hailed as one of the greatest philosophers of all time for nothing) but let's see if we can respond to it step by step:

> *"You desire to LIVE "according to Nature"? Oh, you noble Stoics, what fraud of words! Imagine to yourselves a being like Nature, boundlessly extravagant, boundlessly indifferent, without purpose or consideration, without pity or justice, at once fruitful and barren and uncertain: imagine to yourselves INDIFFERENCE as a power--how COULD you live in accordance with such indifference?"*

This, in my opinion, is the weakest point of the critique. As we've discussed before, this stems from a misunderstanding of Stoicism and its values. It is not indifference that is a power, but rather acceptance, growth, and antifragility.

> *"To live--is not that just endeavoring to be otherwise than this Nature? Is not living valuing, preferring, being unjust, being limited, endeavoring to be different? And granted that your imperative, "living according to Nature," means actually the same as "living according to life"--how could you do DIFFERENTLY? Why should you make a principle out of what you yourselves are, and must be?"*

To be honest, this is an excellent point, depending on our understanding of nature. Nietzsche suffered here because he had grown up in a time when nature had already begun to be understood as "the outside world." In this sense, he is completely right to say that we must live in accordance with nature.

On the other hand, if we take nature as the ideal nature we've talked about before, then suddenly he has much less of a point. Of course, we can live without virtue, countless people already do.

> *"In reality, however, it is quite otherwise with you: while you pretend to read with rapture the canon of your law in Nature, you want something quite the contrary, you extraordinary stage-players and self-deluders! In your pride you wish to dictate your morals and ideals to Nature, to Nature herself, and to incorporate them therein; you insist that it shall be Nature "according to the Stoa," and would like everything to be made after your own*

> *image, as a vast, eternal glorification and generalism of Stoicism!"*

Nietzsche is an excellent writer, but this passage is comprised of mostly insults. In truth, Stoicism does the opposite of this; rather than trying to make nature fit our views, we create our views to reflect nature.

> *"With all your love for truth, you have forced yourselves so long, so persistently, and with such hypnotic rigidity to see Nature FALSELY, that is to say, Stoically, that you are no longer able to see it otherwise--and to crown all, some unfathomable superciliousness gives you the Bedlamite hope that BECAUSE you are able to tyrannize over yourselves--Stoicism is self-tyranny--Nature will also allow herself to be tyrannized over: is not the Stoic a PART of Nature?"*

Here, I believe, Nietzsche is most understandable in his view. He believes that the Stoic way of thinking is self-tyranny and limiting to the human condition. On the other hand, I fail to see how being able to control one's own emotions is self-tyranny. After all, shouldn't maximizing one's own potential be the goal of all humans? Stoicism doesn't repress negativity, rather it serves to steer it and prevent it from ever happening.

> *"But this is an old and everlasting story: what happened in old times with the Stoics still happens today, as soon as ever a philosophy begins to believe in itself. It always creates the world in its own image; it cannot do otherwise; philosophy is this tyrannical impulse itself, the most spiritual Will to Power, the will to "creation of the world," the will to the causa prima."*

This is largely a verbal attack, but it does raise a good question. Is Stoicism only convincing itself reality is in a way which it is not? I would argue this is false, because if it were so, Stoicism would need to adapt swiftly, since its whole point is to be in tune with nature.

PERSONAL PROBLEMS WITH STOICISM

It can sometimes be hard to come to terms with living as a Stoic. Even if you truly believe in the Stoic ideology, it isn't always easy to abide by it.

After all, going from being affected by suffering, to accepting - or even using it - is not a process that can be finished in mere days. I wish I could tell you that once you've finished this book, you'll be able to immediately apply all that it has taught you. Unfortunately, that is not the case. You'll struggle, as does everyone. For most of our lives, we've been taught to live a certain way, and it isn't usually the Stoic way.

Having problems when you first begin living as a Stoic is perfectly normal. Nobody expects you to reach eudaimonia tomorrow (or at all, to be honest). But as long as you're constantly working toward it, you're doing great!

Try to keep in mind the principles and pillars. After all, they are practically the core of Stoic philosophy. They also make it easier to recognize what needs improvement. Rather than just realizing you're having difficulty living as a Stoic, you'll be able to pinpoint your issue(s), and find a fix for them.

You'll be pleased to hear that the next chapter includes exercises for you to do once you're ready to fully make the switch. The most common aspects to have issues with are accepting and avoiding strong emotions. This is even more difficult than not acting on them. Stopping yourself from acting on impulse is the first step. Unfortunately, acceptance and motivation are things you must master for yourself.

MY EXPERIENCE WITH STOICISM

While Stoicism did indeed change my life for the better, it did not happen overnight, nor was it as effortless as reading a book, so I'd like to share a bit about my journey.

Ever since childhood, I was, for lack of a better word, anti-social. I spent most of my time in my room, avoiding other kids, and later on, people. It's not that I didn't like being around people, I would simply become nervous and not know how to behave. I stumbled with my words and would fidget awkwardly.

I was fairly good at school, earning mostly A's without studying much. This led to over-confidence, because when I received my first B in high school, I completely shut down. In the end, I barely graduated. I feel ashamed to admit it, but it really shook me to my core.

After school, I found a low-paying IT chat support job, which paid barely enough for me to live on. I refused to go to college because I was paralyzed by the fear that I would fail again. You see, because I didn't attempt many things, those that I attempted and failed at stayed with me and had a negative effect on my psyche.

I fell into a rut, simply working and browsing the internet 24/7. Out of boredom, I started reading books. Over time, my interests were piqued, and I felt a twinge of enjoyment from reading. This is when I encountered Stoicism. I still remember how I devoured pretty much every Stoic book I could find. Within a few months, I had read all of the influential works of the early Stoics, and I wanted to apply the philosophy to my daily life.

So I tried! I went out with the mission of striking up a conversation with a random person. After all, I couldn't control their reaction, so what was there to be worried about?

But I didn't talk to anyone on that first day. Once again, I felt like a failure, which drove me deeper into the rut I'd dug for myself.

But over time, I started getting better. I used auto-suggestion to convince myself of the value of Stoic principles (this is when you repeat something to yourself so many times, you actually start believing in it).

One day, I was chatting with a group of four people in a bar, and suddenly realized I wasn't fidgeting or tripping over my words. It felt amazing. I eventually began getting promotions, from IT guy, to system administrator, to head of the IT department. Today, I'm an entrepreneur with my own business, and I write on the side.

In all honesty, I can hardly believe that my past, shy self and me today are the same person, and yet here we are. For me, the hardest part of becoming a true Stoic was coming to terms with failure. It was practically impossible for me for much of my early life. The big test was something I had been terrified of for most of my life - asking girls out. But when I got a "no," I realized I didn't care because I'd had plenty of "yes's," so was already quite a bit more confident.

These days, I no longer ask girls out (my wife would not appreciate it). But I still try to fail every now and then, meaning I take risks and try new things. It helps me remember how it feels to fail, as well as how to accept the feelings that come with it and not be fazed by them.

Now I'd like to help you learn this too.

8

PREPARING YOURSELF FOR PRACTICE

The more you know about philosophical schools and their teachings, the richer you will be in your new perspectives and solutions to problems. You may unknowingly change yourself for the better, and you just might find the answers you're looking for. Amazingly, the Stoics thought of problems that equally plague 21st-century humans.

They sought ways to bring peace, fulfillment, happiness, and direction to life. True Stoics are thought to be calm and unwavering people, who tolerate external distress and trouble in a calm and unemotional way. To 'stoically' endure life is virtuous. They were of the opinion that the only way to overcome pain and trouble was to stand up stoically.

In their time, they were highly respected for their moral standards. They appreciated the virtues of reasonableness, righteousness, and moderation, advised that one should live in harmony with nature and one's own reason, and strongly opposed the impulses that create passion, hatred, fear, and pain. To quote Seneca: "It is not one who has a lot that is rich, but one who does not want more than he has."

The Stoics believed that man is a 'free soul' who should despise chance and rejoice in virtue alone. We should nurture the virtues of reason and strive not to be a slave to the body, but to make the body a servant to the mind.

We can enjoy and relate to wealth, position or celebrity, but for the Stoic, these states are a matter of luck, chance or destiny in life. Wealth, fame or status do not depend on the person themselves, so we should be indifferent to such circumstances. The only thing in our power is the care of our own virtue and that is the only thing that matters. Stoics do not reject all of these comforts, but they also do not consider them to be of the highest value and enjoy them in moderation only. Fun fact: Seneca was one of the richest men of his time.

Stoics would also tell you that it is a good idea to consider, 'What's the worst that can happen?' When we imagine losing the people and things that matter most to us, we value what we have and are more grateful.

Contemporary psychologists also endorse the ideas of the Stoics that we need to occasionally discard our daily pleasures in order to appreciate them more when we return to them. This is how willpower and self-discipline are practiced, which build stronger character. (Skip your favorite cake with your favorite coffee for a few days, and then return to them).

And when you make the wrong move, forgive yourself and get back on track. Try again. There is no reason to despair and rebuke yourself. Every fall and subsequent return means you are learning and improving yourself.

After Zeno of Citium survived a shipwreck on a journey from Phoenicia to Peiraeus, he visited a bookshop in Athens. He wasn't expecting anything good to happen. He'd lost everything and didn't have anything much to do, so he went through the books. He found Xenophon's *Memorabilia* and was quickly captivated by the teachings of Socrates. He began searching for the great thinkers and after studying with them, he decided to share his newfound knowledge with those who cared to listen. His teachings were accepted by both slaves and kings.

These teachings remain important and relevant even in modern society and they can bring us calm and peace to face the chaos of every day.

You don't have to turn your life around, just start practicing some of the Stoic principles and apply them to life as best you can. Look to nature and you will better understand the flow of everything. The only source of true wisdom and insight is the experience.

Be mindful in everything you do. This isn't so hard; just remember to be fully present in your life and practice being curious. Enjoy every single bite when you eat.

Apply mindfulness to each of the Stoic practices you find that resonates with you. And practice them, try different approaches. Decide what type of person you want to be and hold onto that. You have the power over your mind to set things into motion and when you realize this, you find your strength. Try to apply this philosophy to every day in the best way you can.

Be aware of every step you take and choose your actions deliberately. Love yourself even when you stumble, because all it means is that you now know where the stumbling blocks are on your path to eudaimonia. You don't have to practice all the principles, just the ones you find will improve the quality of your life.

9

THE PRACTICES

Having done research on many different Stoic practices, I have put together those that will help you face the turmoil of the world.

PRACTICE 1 - DETACHMENT FROM EMOTIONS

When we attach our happiness and existence to our work, our relationships or our family, we are at great risk of losing ourselves. We also develop a strong urge to control external things. We all exercise some control over ourselves, but putting so much of ourselves into something leads us to believe that there is no chance for something to go wrong, thus we live in illusion.

This behavior does not eliminate all the possible risks of things not working out. Feeling too much for something and attaching oneself too strongly leads to not only losing one's sense of self but it also distorts one's reality. We must stay true to the "self" that doesn't depend on anything else in this world. It is yours and it is free.

This can make a huge difference if your life collapses, because as the "self," you can get up, dust yourself off and move forward. Detaching from the emotions means detaching yourself from lesser feelings, so you won't act on impulses led by those emotions. It doesn't mean you have to be detached all the time, but there will be situations in which you wish you could detach, and this is an excellent reason to practice this.

Explore all the possible reasons that can cause you to react with strong emotional impulses. If you want your practice to be successful, you need to be aware of the reason behind any strong emotions. Take note, though: There exists both a healthy and an unhealthy detachment. Extreme emotional detachment from others can be the cause of trauma, and can also be associated with psychopathy. It is not good for our personal growth to emotionally detach in such an extreme way. Everything in moderation is one of the Stoic principles.

Finally, accept your emotions and your current emotional state. All the emotions we feel are completely normal and when we accept them as such, it is easier to detach from them when we need to. We need to practice this detachment because emotions can sometimes cloud our view of reality, and our goal should be to see the truth.

PRACTICE 2 - CONNECT AND CONTROL YOUR EMOTIONS

Emotions are messages from the brain, and to receive these messages we need to feel them as they come. Not feeling an emotion leads us to hold onto it longer and it might grow stronger, causing us to take unconscious actions based on it.

To feel emotion is to be aware of it. To be aware of it is to be able to control it.

Emotions are part of who we are and we cannot run from them. So face them, because facing them means being less afraid of them. Interestingly, acceptance of our emotions is not something we are born with, but a practical skill that requires learning and practice.

PRACTICE 3 - A RISE AND SHINE MORNING CONNECTION WITH YOUR EMOTIONS

As you wake up in the morning, assess your emotions. How do you feel? Do you feel grumpy and not willing to get out of bed? Why?

It could be that you are not happy with your current state in life, and feel depressed. Maybe you just broke up with your significant other or are having family or work issues. But if you practice the mindfulness of your emotions daily, as soon as you wake up, your day will start better and you will feel more positive.

Practicing connection with our emotions in the morning builds a habit of choosing how we want to feel that day. We can choose to feel happy each morning.

PRACTICE 4 - A BEFORE-BED DETACHMENT

Your day has come to an end and you are preparing for bed. Think about your day. How did you feel throughout it? Could you have reacted differently to some situations?

Go through your emotions and the reason for them. Determine what triggered them and why you felt the way you did. Accept all the emotions as they are - feel them. Then realize that each emotion likely rose in the spur of the moment and that you probably didn't have to feel the way you did.

PRACTICE 5 - SIMPLY OBSERVE YOUR EMOTIONS

Sit down and identify the emotion you are feeling. You might be feeling a mixture of emotions, but identify the most prominent one. Write it down on a piece of paper. Give that emotion a shape, size and color: envision it.

When you give an emotion these attributes, it is easier to see it as it is inside of you. And this is the most important thing - seeing the things as they really are so we can more easily deal with them.

Finally, reflect on that image of the emotion. Did your view of it change? Was the emotion more or less scary? This might be difficult at first, but as you practice it from day to day, it will become easier to accept the emotions you feel.

PRACTICE 6 - INSTANTLY CHANGE YOUR EMOTION AT THE MOMENT IT ARRIVES

If somebody says something hurtful to us, we usually feel the urge to hurt them back. But it is unnecessary to feel hurt. In an instant, you can choose not to feel hurt. Decide that what the other person said has nothing to do with you, but with how they perceive you, and that is something you cannot control. People see what they choose to see. And just like that, it no longer has a meaning to you, as you have utilized self-control. Everything you hear is not a fact, no matter how benevolent or harmful it may seem. The universe changes constantly, as do we.

PRACTICE 7 - INSTANTLY DETACH FROM YOUR EMOTION AT THE MOMENT IT ARRIVES

It sounds difficult, but if you can calm your thoughts and take a step back and breathe, you'll feel the emotions, but realize they don't have control over your actions. Think about what the *calm you* would do, how the calm you would respond to the emotional trigger. And is the emotion important or is it just in the moment? If it is important, you need to proceed with constructive thinking so you can make the best decision. If it is merely an emotion in the spur of the moment, let it pass. There is no need to be overwhelmed by simple matters in life and spend your energy on things that don't benefit you.

PRACTICE 8 - A MORNING STOIC ROUTINE

> *"When you first rise in the morning tell yourself: I will encounter busybodies, ingrates, egomaniacs, liars, the jealous and cranks. They are all stricken with these afflictions because they don't know the difference between good and evil."*
>
> *— MARCUS AURELIUS*

Take the time to look inward, use the practices we have discussed, examine and reflect. Do this in the morning as you wake up and at night before you go to bed. You need to prepare yourself for what you might encounter. This exercise is not about preparing yourself to go against everyone, but it is preparation for what you might encounter and how to reasonably act.

Not everyone is as well prepared as you will be. Train yourself to expect everything and be ready for anything. This little morning preparation is important if you want to keep your calm and focus while being the best you can be.

PRACTICE 9 - MENTALLY SET UP YOUR MINDSET FOR THE DAY

Overcoming obstacles and hurdles, accepting whatever happens and having no fear of what's ahead is part of being a Stoic.

You can start each day by envisioning how you are going to deal with the chaos of the day. Prepare yourself for anything you might encounter with no fear of it. Some things just happen, but when you stay calm and collected, you can find a way to deal with anything.

Practice, so you can look at adversity in the eye and see an idea or potential instead of a challenge. It will take time to get there, but the results are rewarding. Start thinking about how every question has an answer and how every problem has a solution. Or just think about how you can turn the uncomfortable situation you are in to your advantage. There is nothing you can't handle.

PRACTICE 10 - VIEW EVERYTHING AS IT IS LENT FROM NATURE

The Stoics believed the Universe has its own nature, and everything in that nature is connected and interchangeable.

Everything inside your own mind and body is part of that nature, as well as anything or anyone you encounter throughout life. So, everything that happens comes from nature, which means you can handle everything that comes your way. Everything is part of the same flow.

PRACTICE 11 - UNDERTAKE ACTION WITH A STOIC MINDSET

To undertake an action with a Stoic mindset means to do the best you can. It means to carry out an action with reason and confidence. Take action with no fear, because the outcome is not in your control. How well you perform the action, on the other hand, is in your control, so strive to do everything to the best of your abilities.

Keeping the Stoic mindset means to be present in the moment and to see the reality of things, not be bothered by outside circumstances. Practice being here and now, and doing your best for today.

PRACTICE 12 - UNDERSTAND, ACCEPT AND REMIND YOURSELF OF THE IMPERMANENCE OF EVERYTHING

Nothing in this life is permanent, not even our life. And we have to make peace with that. It is what it is. Time is passing, we will not be young forever and we will not be alive for a thousand years. So, it is time to take action now. Practice mindfulness and do everything with a sense of purpose. It can only benefit you and help you thrive.

PRACTICE 13 - RESPONSE TO GRIEF

> *"It is better to conquer our grief than to deceive it. For if it has withdrawn, being merely beguiled by pleasures and preoccupations, it starts up again and from its very respite gains force to savage us. But the grief that has been conquered by reason is calmed forever. I am not, therefore, going to prescribe for you those remedies which I know many people have used, that you divert or cheer yourself by a long or pleasant journey abroad, or spend a lot of time carefully going through your accounts and administering your estate, or constantly be involved in some new activity. All those things help only for a short time; they do not cure grief but hinder it. But I would rather end it than distract it."*

— SENECA

We are all mortal. People around us will die and it will hurt us. The question for us, as it was for the Stoic, is how we can make sense of this. Grief is a very powerful emotion and it may be tempting to avoid it. But that is not an option in Stoic teachings. Practice awareness and understanding of what happened. This means facing it and defining what you are feeling. Remove any feeling of being wronged and sit with your pain and accept it. Remember this is part of life and we must come to terms with our grief.

PRACTICE 14 - RESPONSE TO PRAISE

> *"You can tell the character of every man when you see how he gives and receives praise."*

— SENECA

The way we receive praise says a lot about our reason behind our action. Those who seek praise are expecting validation from others so they can justify themselves or their existence. But according to Stoicism, this means they are letting the opinions of others affect their actions.

We do not need praise from others to feel complete. What we want and need is praise from ourselves. Your opinion is something you can control. We need to know we did the right thing in accordance with nature and that we are pleased with it.

PRACTICE 15 - RESPONSE TO RESPECT

To Stoics, self-respect is one of the virtues. Why? Because when you respect yourself, you will never do anything to lose that respect. And interestingly, if you do things that are just and right, your self-respect will grow. And when you are always doing your best, what is there not to be respected? Stoic philosophy teaches us not to do things for the approval of others, so practice doing the right and reasonable thing in any situation for your own sense of self-respect.

PRACTICE 16 - RESPONSE TO DISRESPECT AND THE LEVEL OF DISRESPECT BEFORE YOU RESPOND

> *"To be like the rock that the waves keep crashing over. It stands unmoved and the raging of the sea falls still around it."*
>
> — *MARCUS AURELIUS*

Pause and consider why disrespect is even taking place. If someone has a reason to disrespect you, there is no point in getting upset. If they are showing disrespect and they are not familiar with your character, educate them with patience and calm.

You could respond with humor, as Stoics sometimes did. For example, Epictetus once suggested that someone obviously didn't know him well enough or they would have mentioned more damning flaws in his character. You might also offer no response at all, depriving the one who showed you disrespect of the pleasure of upsetting you.

But there are times when you just have to respond to disrespect, as in the example of a student insulting a teacher. A teacher cannot allow disruptive behavior, so they must set boundaries with their response. This is for the greater good and preserving peace. And the teacher is punishing bad behavior to correct it, not to get even.

PRACTICE 17 - ORGANIZE YOURSELF AND SET YOUR PRIORITIES

Productivity is very important to every human being and it was important for the Stoics. By organizing our lives we are reducing the chances for chaos to occur or of losing time. It is about self-control and applying that control to the time we have.

We have certain tasks and a certain amount of time to get them done. So practicing your organizational skills throughout your day would be a very Stoic thing to do, as it makes you more focused and productive.

Set your goals and firmly decide to go after them. Determine your priorities. If you have an exam but a birthday party the day before the exam, which is more important to you? As we discussed earlier in this book, these are different roles and the key is in balancing them. You are exchanging one value for another, but which is more important for your betterment?

PRACTICE 18 - CUT OUT THE IRRELEVANT: SOCIAL MEDIA, ETC., AND TAKE YOUR TIME

We all have distractions, but for many in today's culture, they have taken over our lives. Exercise self-control by being mindful of how much time you waste every day scrolling through apps on your phone. You are not relaxing nor working on your own betterment.

Take time for yourself and enjoy it. There are great ways you could spend what little free time you have. Draw a relaxing bath, go for a run, cook a meal or read a book.

This all benefits you on a much higher level. It will make you feel accomplished and your levels of stress and anxiety will be enormously reduced, as opposed to spending too much time on things like social media, which has been proven to increase stress and anxiety.

PRACTICE 19 - KEEP A ROLE MODEL IN MIND AND REMIND YOURSELF OF THEM TO ACHIEVE YOUR OWN SUCCESS

Throughout life, we often come to know of people whom we admire and respect. If you have a good role model in your life, that is even better. When dealing with difficult situations or other people, ask yourself, what would my role model do or how would they handle the situation at hand?

Sometimes we assign our role models better characteristics than they actually possess, but this practice is still helpful to us, as it leads us to recognize the right thing to do. So try keeping in mind that person or tyoe of person whenever you are facing an obstacle in life.

PRACTICE 20 - VISUALIZE THE NEGATIVE, FORESEEING THE WORST THAT COULD HAPPEN

By visualizing the negative, the Stoics prepared their minds for what might happen. Try it. Think about the worst-case scenario or everything that could go wrong. It is scary at first. But as you practice this, you will notice that you become calmer when dealing with problems and that you have strengthened your mind to find the solution on the spot.

This will ensure that not many things can take you by surprise or paralyze you with fear. It enables you to take action whenever it is needed and opens you up to possibilities.

PRACTICE 21 - VISUALIZE THE POSITIVE, FORESEEING THE BEST THAT COULD HAPPEN

Now visualize the best that could happen. You need to remind yourself of the splendid and wonderful things that are part of this life, so they also don't take you by surprise. This practice helps you to not be swept away by positive feelings, and to remain calm and take reasonable actions. This will help the positive to last.

PRACTICE 22 - REVIEW YOUR DAY TO IMPROVE YOUR NEXT

Think about your day. What were the positives and what were the negatives? Consider why you view them in such a manner and what you could do to make these things not affect you as much.

Learn from each day; there is always something we can correct or improve that will make our next day easier.

AFTERWORD

This is the end of our journey together, but it isn't the end of yours. We've barely dipped our toes into the infinite depths of Stoicism. If this book has sparked the same interest in you as it did in me years ago, then I consider it a job well done.

Let's recap some of the most important things we've covered:

The foundation of Stoicism

Stoicism was founded by Zeno of Citium, and is divided into early, middle, and late stoa phases. The late stoa is mainly Roman, and is dominated by ethics, rather than logic and physics, which used to be considered just as important.

The pursuit of eudaimonia

Eudaimonia—or well-being, enlightenment, flourishing, etc., is achieved through the pursuit of virtue. Since wisdom is considered the ultimate virtue, this is done through reason. One of the most important aspects of this pursuit is the ability to ignore the influence of the external, and not let it affect us internally.

The principles and pillars of Stoicism

Stoicism rests upon several principles and pillars.

The principles interweave together to describe the world of the Stoic, from its lawful nature, to the reason we need to fight against passionate emotions - because they get in the way of the pursuit of eudaimonia by clouding rational thought.

The pillars describe the behavior of the Stoic, ranging from their ability to accept intense emotions and even turn them into fuel, to the duty to take action to achieve justice and virtue.

Poverty, illness, and death are not evil

The idea that these conditions that plague humankind are not evil is hard to comprehend. But if we consider them from a Stoic perspective, they are all a direct consequence of the natural order of things, an order by which the Stoic must abide. It is imperative that we learn to accept these things, as they exist because of human nature and natural law.

How a Stoic approaches death

Marcus Aurelius teaches us that the best way to greet death is much like it greets us - with a smile. Death is not something to be worried about, rather, we should worry about things that are in our power to change. Out of all external things, death is the least within our grasp to influence. As Epictetus would say:

> *"I have to die. If it is now, well then I die now; if later, then now I will take my lunch, since the hour for lunch has arrived - and dying I will tend to later."*

The mindset of a Stoic

In chapter 5, we went into great detail about the Stoic mindset, and analyzed Stoic perspectives on countless things. If I had to pick a chapter from this book that was the most vital for you to review, it would be this one, because it offers the most value, and the most teachings for you to master.

Business and Stoicism

We've also gone over how Stoicism can help your career, and how it has been linked not only to being a successful entrepreneur, but also investor, or even worker. We drew parallels between the behavior of the world's richest people and those of Stoics. We also discussed how best to position yourself in your professional life according to Stoicism, whether it be as an entrepreneur or a worker.

Critiques of Stoicism

In chapter 7 are the most well-known counterarguments against Stoicism. Some, if not most of them, have probably gone through your head while reading this book. If so, that is good, it is the nature of a Stoic to question things and approach them with reason, rather than trusting blindly.

We also talked about me in this chapter. I told you about things I struggled with as a young man, as well as how Stoicism helped me climb out of the dark place I was in.

Finally, we talked about how it's perfectly fine to struggle a bit while attaining a Stoic mindset. After all, nobody is born a sage.

Practices

We ended the book on a practical note, with 22 practices that you can engage in to train yourself to become a better Stoic. These range from simple to complex, but all have the same goal: to instill a Stoic mindset not only in your conscious thought, but also your subconscious.

The subconscious mind is a powerful thing, so by instilling it with your ideals, you gain ultimate control over yourself and your own fate. If there was only one thing to remember from this book, it is this:

Never stop improving yourself, and never stop reaching for eudaimonia, no matter how unattainable it may seem!

Printed in Great Britain
by Amazon